Date Due

May 27 '63			
JUN 29 1962			
JUL 11 1967			
JUL 13 1967			
Aug 4, 1975			
OCT 16 1975			
APR 26 1977			
APR 28 1978			
MAR 26 1980			
SEP 19 1995			
AUG 14 2003			

PAR GOLF FOR WOMEN

Par Golf for Women

Louise Suggs

NEW YORK PRENTICE-HALL, INC.

L.C. Cat. Card No.: 53-7114

Contents

Foreword

THE FIRST TIME I EVER SAW LOUISE SUGGS HIT A GOLF BALL WAS IN 1945 when we were partners in a pro-lady event preceding the Chicago Victory Open. It was on the tough No. 3 course at Medinah where the National Open was played four years later.

Louise and I won that pro-lady competition. And after I'd watched her fine shot-making at Medinah, to me her later victories in the U. S. Women's and the Women's Western Championships and her triumph in every other major championship in the United States and in the British Ladies' Championship, as well, seemed the logical result. The swing she showed in 1945 was a beautiful thing – so smooth and rhythmic, so soundly joined together – she was bound to be a winner.

If I were to single out one woman in the world today as a model for any other woman aspiring to ideal golf form, it would be Miss Suggs. Her swing combines all the desirable elements of efficiency, timing, and coordination. It appears to be completely effortless. Yet, despite her slight build, she is consistently as long off the tee and through the fairway as any of her feminine contemporaries in competitive golf. And no one is "right down the middle" any more than this sweet-swinging Georgia miss.

Her game shows the benefits of a great deal of intelligent experimenting, study, and practice. Her timing and her consistently high standard of play stay with her for the reason that she's gotten the fundamentals and the refinements down to where they reduce the margin of error to about its minimum.

I know Louise to be a particularly keen student of golf and have always been impressed with her sound concepts of the game. Her thinking in regard to good golf form is simple and basic. It is completely practical and free of the frills and theories that tend only to make a complex action of the golf swing.

Because of this clear thinking and strictly fundamental approach to the process of stroking a golf ball with maximum efficiency, Louise is able to impart to others these proven principles in thoroughly understandable terms.

Anyone sincerely interested in playing golf well cannot help benefiting from the wealth of advice and instruction presented so ably by Miss Suggs in the pages that follow. The text and the scores of excellent illustrations combine to do the best instructional and informational job I have yet encountered in the vastly expanding field of women's golf.

BEN HOGAN

Introduction

THE MORE GOLF CLINICS I GIVE, THE MORE I BECOME CONVINCED THAT although the average player has a sincere desire to improve her game, she becomes too easily discouraged before she has given herself an even break. She is too anxious to see good results on the scoreboard before she has fully absorbed the principles of the golf swing in mind and muscle on the practice tee.

It may appear obvious, but the only answer I can give to the eternal question "What actually makes your game tick, Louise?" is that I attempt first of all to understand what it is that I am trying to do. To this end, I work on the practice tee to coordinate my muscles until I get a feeling of naturalness and freedom in my swing. Finally, I venture out on the course which is my proving ground.

I think that any seasoned player will agree that she is at her best golfwise when her determination to swing properly at the ball outweighs her anxiety to send the ball off to some particular spot. When a player reaches the point where she can stand up to a shot and say, "I am going to execute as perfect a swing as I know how, regardless of where the ball goes," she will realize the most from her efforts. This shift of concentration from the flight of the ball to the swing itself requires a working knowledge of the fundamentals of the golf swing. The locker rooms vibrate with phrases such as "braced left side" and "forward press." But to attempt to incorporate these scattered ideas into the swing is futile.

I cannot overemphasize the importance of working with the professional at this point. The player whose head is bursting with a disconnected picture of a thousand details in the golf swing is defeated at the start, for one mind cannot send so many different messages to so many parts of the body during an uninterrupted motion such as the swing. The player discovers, however, that in practice supervised by her professional, these mechanical details gradually work themselves into an integrated whole.

The second phase in building a sound golf game — that of coordinating the muscles with the correct mental picture of the swing — is too often overlooked by Mrs. Average Player. She probably does not have all the time in the world to spend at the club, and after all, her main interest is to spend as much of that time as possible on the course with her favorite foursome. Yet I have found that it does me more harm than good to attempt to work out flaws in my swing on the course. It is continual repetition of the correct swing and the ability for complete concentation which count here, and I think that the practice tee and a bucket of balls are the ideal setting at this stage of the game.

The real value of such workouts on the practice tee is that in this way, the player is able to build up her concentration, her confidence, and a trust in her own particular swing which she never would have thought possible. She also discovers that these practice sessions become almost as enjoyable as playing. Undisciplined practice, however, is at the root of many an unwanted habit in the golf swing. I guard against hitting practice shots in a careless and haphazard manner by concentrating on shooting for a specific spot and by focusing my attention to execute as nearly perfect a swing as I possibly can on each shot. When my mind begins to wander, or when I am satisfied that I have found the feeling in my swing which I have been seeking, I quit. I know that I have had enough for the time being.

Confident that she has gained some understanding of the golf swing, and encouraged by the knowledge that she has progressed to some extent in putting these ideas into practice, the player is better prepared both mentally and physically to try out her theories on the course itself.

In short, it seems to me that the average player will find that this game of golf will assume a new fascination and a new satisfaction for her as she develops a curiosity as to what actually "makes the swing go 'round."

I

Women Are Golfers, Too

GOLF IS AN IDEAL FORM OF EXERCISE FOR WOMEN BECAUSE IN PLAYING it, they can set the pace for themselves. Few, if any, other forms of sport or recreation afford the companionship of sociability to be found by women on the golf course.

The woman who plays golf properly and according to the rules is bound to improve her own qualities of sportsmanship, for the game affords good opportunity for emotional control. The time that expires between shots gives the player time in which to calm down and do some clear thinking. By playing the game, the married woman or the girl who is about to be married reduces the chances of becoming a "golf widow," for today, there is a very commendable trend toward "family days" and mixed competition at the country clubs across the nation. This is a time when husband and wife may mingle with their golfing friends in a very pleasant association and activity. The better the game of golf played by the feminine portion of these mixed groups, the greater the enjoyment of all.

The notion that women have inherent physical limitations restricting them in golf has been completely discredited. It is a game that can be enjoyed by women of almost any physical proportions or muscular development. In a Women's National Amateur Golf championship some years ago, a tall slender girl of supposedly very limited strength and "natural" athletic ability defeated a very husky, sturdy rival with many important championships to her credit. Though it may be a surprise to some, golf is *not* a game of power and brute strength. It is a matter of grace, rhythm, finesse, and timing. These are qualities that very few women cannot develop if they make a serious effort to do so. A smaller person using a good swing will nearly always hit the ball past a larger person relying entirely on brute strength to power the ball.

I have heard it said that women are naturally emotionally unsuited for golf. This notion has already been so thoroughly discredited that it is scarcely worth consideration. The championship golfers of today by no means follow a single pattern. Most of them get "butterflies" in their stomachs before engaging in a competitive match, but this is also true of the top male golfers.

Since most women lack the vanity of men about athletic prowess, they are more inclined to realize their physical limitations and to try to offset them by improving their game through qualified instruction. Furthermore, it is almost second nature with girls and women to be graceful in their movements, for this is something that is drilled into them as a desirable, lady-like quality from the time they are small. In this respect, they have an advantage over men, for the rhythmic motion that is the essence of a good golf swing is learned more easily.

You are never too old to play golf. If you can walk, you can play. On the other hand, it seems impossible to be too young, for we have examples of girls today who started swinging miniature clubs at the age of 3. My personal feeling is that this is too young. I doubt that youngsters of this age can grasp the mechanism of a golf swing, and they certainly lack the coordination and the necessary strength. Because of this, golf becomes an effort for them. This should not be.

I feel that 10 years is young enough. By this time most girls are out of the "doll stage" and have experienced some competitive activity. Chances are they have developed a sense of timing, and it is no longer a struggle for them to handle a golf club. Most manufacturers today produce junior sets of golf clubs intended for children of approximately eight and over; they don't make them for children any younger. At the age of 10 a youngster is capable of reasoning and taking instruction, although he may need some encouragement from his parents if he is to take the game seriously and accept it as a regular recreational activity.

Women vs. Men As Golfers

I would be the last person to contend that the top women golfers could ever match scores with an equal number of the top male golfers. The men just simply have too much length off the tee and through the fairway where woods and long irons are required. But in my opinion, a woman really comes into her own in matching a man within 125 yards of the cup.

The value of being long off the tee and through the fairway on the par five holes and long par four holes was brought home to me very vividly in a mixed two-ball tournament at Orlando, Florida, in which I was paired with Toney Penna, one of the high-ranking professionals. This was a selective drive, alternate shot event. Toney could scarcely believe his eyes when he added up the card and found that we had shot a 65 from the men's tees. Naturally we had selected most of Toney's drives. Some of my shots to the green were so close that Toney apologized for missing the putts that were left him.

Because the short game is the low-scoring hope of women, it is on this department that we must concentrate. That scores in the low seventies are commonplace in the major women's open events today, with an occasional card in the high 60's showing up, is indicative of the proficiency that women are achieving around the greens and in accuracy off the tees and through the fairways with their woods and long irons.

By today's standards in women's professional golf, I am not considered a long hitter. I do get good distance for my height (5 feet 5½ inches) and weight (115 pounds). Despite the fact that I do not get my tee shots out with the longest drivers, I was able to shoot a 68 in the qualifying round of a recent Women's Western Open played over the Whitemarsh Valley Country Club in Philadelphia. Play was from the men's tees. This score was achieved through *accuracy* and *consistency* — factors just as much within the grasp of women as men.

I mention this because I believe that I am about average in size and strength for a young woman. What I have achieved in golf is certainly not beyond the reach of any other woman who enjoys the game as much as I do and is willing to put as much time and effort in to it. Golf has never been drudgery for me. Recently, when I experienced great shock and sorrow, I found that golf afforded me a means of escape and a release for nervous energy. I have never permitted the game to become a chore. I play or practice only because I want to. The benefits I have derived from playing golf have subsequently made it very attractive to me, though I never hoped for them when I started.

Advice vs. Instruction

The one *sure* way to develop a sound golf game is to seek *competent* instruction from the outset. The beginner in golf is usually deluged with all kinds of well-meant advice (usually erroneous) following the announcement that he or she intends to take up the game. Chances are that the people rendering all these words of "wisdom" are in no way qualified to teach others, or have ever even taken the trouble to expose themselves to authentic instructions. I very definitely feel that the best investment anyone can make in time, effort, and money, insofar as golf is concerned, is good instruction from a qualified professional instructor.

Don't be impressed by fancy phrases and theories; they tend to confuse rather than clarify. The *simple, basic* approach to golf is the best.

You must have confidence in your instructor. Don't hesitate to ask him to clarify any point that is not perfectly clear to you. It's a serious mistake to be timid and to fear that you may "show your ignorance." If you want to get the maximum advantage from instruction, be a *good listener.* Don't be impatient to get at that ball and slug it. Bide your time, taking one step at a time until you are at last at the stage where you can step up to a shot with full confidence. Indecisiveness is a serious impediment to golfing achievement. It is a bugaboo that haunts all too many players. Confidence is the only antidote.

An important part of your training is to learn to "play within yourself." By this I mean that you should never extend yourself in an attempt to force a shot. Don't let false pride lead you to try to get more distance out of a club than can be ordinarily expected of one of your physical ability. To concern yourself with what the "other fellow" is doing in the way of distance or scoring is complete folly. Just concentrate on yourself.

It is really unfortunate that so many people begin golf with apprehension, misgivings, and a confused mind. These individuals have no doubt heard countless tales of woe encountered on the golf course. They have been parties to or listeners-in at many discussions over the seeming complexity and futility of the game. This is absolutely the wrong approach. You should start out with the idea that you can master this sport. Anyone with average mentality, normal senses, and lacking a serious physical deficiency CAN play golf well.

An incident that occurred during my childhood comes to mind as an example of the right mental attitude for a beginner.

My grandfather, who was then in his early fifties, had always seen golf played by comparatively low-handicap golfers. Though he had never in his life even hit a golf ball, he thought it must be a simple matter. The complainers and "groaners" whom he had heard on occasion could not change the conviction that he had developed through observing good golfers in action. He was at the club one day for lunch when he saw a group of friends about to tee off. He walked over to these people and immediately began to chide them about the relative simplicity of golf. In the course of some good-natured ribbing he exclaimed, "Listen, I have never so much as swung at a golf ball, but I'll bet I can hit it as far as any one of you." The challenge was accepted. Sure enough, he hit the ball straight down the fairway about 215 yards, much to the amazement of the members of the foursome.

I bring up this incident to show just how significant confidence can be. My grandfather was convinced that there was nothing to hitting a golf ball. This initial and successful experience led him to take up the game seriously. The combination of self-assurance and good instruction, which was well-heeded on his part, led him to become a better than average player in a short time. He had many scores in the low 80's and high 70's.

My own training in golf was simple and direct. My Dad, who was and is my teacher, believed in schooling me only in the basic fundamentals of golf, with emphasis on timing and accuracy. Like my Dad, I feel that good instruction omits the many trivialities that serve only to confuse the mind of the pupil. Minor technicalities should be considered only as one achieves an advanced degree of proficiency. Concern yourself solely with the basic fundamentals as you begin your golfing education.

Group Instruction

Private or individual instruction is not the only means of acquiring a knowledge of the basic principles of golf. Many men and women today are getting a very good start in golf through group instruction. Large companies with an employee recreation plan, have started such programs as have colleges and universities where classes are conducted as a part of the physical education curriculum. Most of the larger cities make group instruction available through their municipal or park recreation programs.

Your Objectives in Golf

It is wise when you arrive at the stage where you become intent on playing golf seriously to decide just what you expect to get out of golf and what you are willing to put into it to achieve your aim.

If you are ever to become an accomplished competitive golfer, you must have within yourself strong desire to improve yourself and to excel at the game. At the same time you must be willing to sacrifice a little in irregular hours and dissipation. It is not meant that you can no longer have fun and enjoy occasional deviations from a rigid training routine. And I don't mean that you have to be completely grim in your approach to the game. Golf is primarily a recreation, but when it is played competitively, it calls for intense application and concentration. I personally have found the game a constant source of pleasure and satisfaction. Through overindulgence you can become stale. When this happens I just simply "lay off" for a few days until I feel the urge to play calling me back to the practice tee or the course.

A *good* game of golf, unlike fame or fortune, is something you cannot acquire by accident. You can't wish or dream yourself into pars and birdies. Neither can you buy a consistently-sound game. You excel only as you apply yourself. Not even the best instruction in the world can help if you are not willing to put it to practical use, and to exercise the care so essential to profiting from this instruction.

It is said that once a person acquires sound golfing form, it never leaves him completely. However, all the prominent professionals agree that they do become rusty if they stay away from the game any more than a few days at a time, timing and "feel" being the first to suffer.

Again I say, if you intend to become proficient at the game of golf, you must have desire and tenacity. Without these qualities, no one can possibly rise above mediocrity.

Please bear this in mind – the most certain way to enjoy golf is to play it well. I have often wondered why so many people limit the pleasure they derive from the game by being satisfied with playing it so poorly, and making no effort toward improvement. This applies to many people who play the game regularly and frequently. Unfortunately their approach to the game is haphazard and unsystematic. They are intent only on getting the ball into the cup, with no regard for the efficiency with which they do so.

These people comprise the great army of so-called "hackers" and "duffers" who will not seek qualified advice to correct the golfing ills that plague them.

It has always seemed strange to me that the same industrial tycoon who calls in a high-paid business engineering firm to seek and remedy inefficiencies in his business, makes himself miserable on the golf course, hour after hour, year after year, lacking the good sense to get his troubles on the course ironed out through the simple expedient of spending a few hours under the eye of a teaching professional. Chances are this same individual has made a very large investment in membership, dues, and equipment, yet he is unwilling to spend a little time, application, and money on the one thing that could bring him the greatest return of all from his golfing endeavors – the satisfaction and pleasure that come with the ability to play well and consistently.

All too many people think they can straighten out their own golf game through self-criticism and self-instruction. This is impossible. Even the great Bobby Jones, who stands today as a symbol of golfing perfection and achievement, was constantly under the watchful eye of the late Stewart Maiden. As astute as Jones was at the height of his competitive career, he could not always put his finger on the cause of troubles that occasionally showed up in his swing. However, he was shrewd enough to refuse to indulge in the vexing process of trying to cure his swinging ills through trial and error (self-cure). He refused to worry when a little off his game, for he had supreme confidence that his instructor was thoroughly competent to detect the cause of the trouble and correct it.

2

Some Advice Before You Play

TO GET THE MAXIMUM IN PLEASURE AND SATISFACTION OUT OF YOUR golfing activities, it is very important that you be courteous and extend full consideration to other people on the course while playing. The best way to accomplish this is to acquaint yourself thoroughly with the rules, regulations, and etiquette of the game. The hour or so it might take to learn the rules of golf will pay back big dividends in enjoyment of the game. There is nothing complicated about the rules, but an understanding of them can increase your over-all pleasure in the game.

The Etiquette of Golf

The "etiquette" of golf is a series of ten suggestions that has nothing to do with the rules, but merely points out certain standards of behavior that will make golf more pleasant for everybody on the course. Caddies are expected to know the etiquette, so that their behavior is as gentlemanly as the golfers for whom they are caddying.

(1) No one should move or talk or stand close to or directly behind the ball or the hole when a player is making a stroke.

(2) The player who has the honor should be allowed to play before his opponent tees his ball.

(3) No player should play until the people in the party ahead are out of range.

(4) When the result of a hole has been determined, players should immediately leave the putting green.

(5) Players while looking for a lost ball should allow other matches coming up to pass them; they should signal to the players following them to pass, and having given such a signal, they should

not continue their play until these players have passed and are out of range.

(6) A player should see that any turf cut or displaced by him is at once replaced and pressed down.

(7) Players should carefully fill up all holes made in a bunker.

(8) Players should see that their caddies do not injure the holes by standing close to them when the ground is soft or in replacing the flagstick.

(9) A player who has incurred a penalty should indicate the fact to his opponent as soon as possible.

(10) Players should at all times play without undue delay.

Displays of temper reveal weakness of character, and make you appear ridiculous to others. You also make it hard for yourself when you "blow your top." Control of emotions is one of the most important achievements to be gained in your golf schooling. The best attitude on the golf course is to forget immediately the shot you just hit – good or bad – and think about the next one. Most of today's great golfers follow this practice unerringly. Anyone fuming and fussing about a shot that went bad cannot possibly give proper thought and attention to the next one. The more angry one allows himself to get over poor shots, the less rational he actually becomes. Efficiency and pleasure decrease proportionately as anger increases.

While golf is basically a sociable game affording splendid opportunity to make and develop friendships, it must of necessity be played on a different basis when the elements of competition and winning enter in. This does not refer to the friendly weekday foursome involving a small wager, but to important tournament play. If you are playing golf "for keeps," it is necessary to concentrate completely upon each shot you play. This cannot be done if one is chatting freely and paying attention to others around him. Many of today's top competitive players are often unjustly criticized for their seeming coolness toward the galleries. Well-meaning galleryites who try to engage a player in conversation are sometimes put out by the lack of response from that player. These individuals fail to appreciate the strain under which big-time tournament players operate. If you will observe these same "cool, calculating" players when they are giving an exhibition or demonstration, or are relaxing off the course, you will usually find them to have entirely different personalities.

To the best of my knowledge, no golfer who has failed to develop his powers of concentration to an extremely high degree has even become a consistent winner in important amateur, professional, or open competition.

Very few less-accomplished golfers realize that many of their bad shots are the result of failure to think out the problem at hand. Yet much of anyone's golf game is played (or should be played) in that short "six-inch course between the ears." There are scores of relatively unknown golfers today who can swing a club every bit as well as the "name" professionals, but the big difference is that they just don't use their heads as efficiently. Many prominent golfers will tell you that most people could improve their game simply by using *common sense* each time they step up to play a shot. This shouldn't be so difficult, should it? But strangely enough, all too few golfers below the championship level follow this rule.

Equipment

In the matter of equipment, it is again the best practice to seek the advice of someone who is qualified to help you select golf implements best suited to you personally. The common procedure of going to the attic or basement for castoffs when someone in the family takes up the game is definitely the wrong approach. This immediately handicaps the beginner. Chances are that the clubs will be unsuited as to weight, length, and grip size. It's a good bet, too, that they are outmoded clubs that may not even comply with today's regulations. Unless it is a matter of economic necessity, the beginned should not be handicapped with poor equipment. Here again the matter of confidence enters in. As we mentioned earlier, this is a vital factor in playing golf well.

One of the most significant advances that has been made in golf in the past 20 years is the improvement in playing equipment. All manufacturers now offer a wide selection in quality, price, design, weight, shaft tension, and length. Consequently it is a simple matter to find woods and irons that are suited to most individual needs. The many fine medium and moderately-priced clubs on the market make it unnecessary to buy the most expensive equipment.

Clothing must also be selected with thought. One of many reasons that women are playing better golf today than they did 20 years ago is that they are wearing clothes better suited to participation in active sports. Any garment that restricts motion is a handicap. There are many manufacturers today who feature practical yet stylish sportswear, much of which is reasonably priced.

Firm footing is another essential. There are any number of comfortable yet attractive golf shoes on the market. Ordinary play shoes are not suitable. Only spiked or lug-soled shoes give you the necessary stability that is so important in keeping proper balance. You need slip only as much as a quarter of an inch to throw your entire swing off.

The Process of Learning

The most important factor in becoming an accomplished golfer is the URGE to play the game and to play it well. Hand-in-hand with this urge or desire must go the willingness to listen intently and to assimilate the knowledge that is being imparted to you. The best instruction in the world is of no consequence if you fail to grasp the significance of what you are being told. The mere act of *teaching* does not necessarily imply that there is *learning* on the part of the individual being taught. You must be completely receptive.

Be sure that you understand every detail of what you are being told by your golf instructor. Don't hesitate to ask questions if a point is not clear to you. If you do not have the entire picture of the golf swing, you cannot acquire the confidence that is so very essential.

Once your program of instruction is under way and you know clearly in your own mind just what you are trying to accomplish, it is imperative that you put into practice what you have learned. Here again desire plays an important role. If you really *want* to become a good golfer, you will not have to force yourself to practice. In fact it will take little or no effort. You will find, when your mental approach to the game is right, that you really get a "kick" out of practice and the progress that goes with it. For these reasons it is a sad error to try to *force* anyone to play golf. Unless the game itself and the learning and practicing that go with it are attractive to an individual, there can be little hope of future success.

Some people have the mistaken impression that I was forced into golf because my father is a teaching golf professional. Such is far from the case. My Dad paid little or no attention to me until after I had been hitting at the ball for three or four years. Then, when I was about 14, he realized that I truly liked the game, and would consequently be receptive to teaching and to the practical application of his teaching. He didn't want to waste any time on me until he was convinced that I really *wanted* to learn to play golf and stay with it.

It must be admitted that there is a factor of tediousness in the learning process. The golf swing is not a *natural* physical motion. It seems at times that one is making little or no progress. Then all of a sudden you "catch on." At no time did my Dad have to tell me to practice. I was always eager to practice because it meant progress to me, and with progress comes immense personal satisfaction.

How to Start

There are several schools of thought as to the proper time to start golf education. There are some people who maintain that instruction should start right at the outset. Others believe that you should "play on your own" for a while.

It is my belief that age is the determining factor in choosing between these two approaches to the game. In the case of youngsters of grade school and high school age I believe it is best to let them go along on their own and "set their own pace," so to speak, though it is well to make sure that the youngster knows how to grip the club properly. Of course the boy who caddies will have some advantages for he is being exposed more directly to golf and is apt to develop more than monetary interest. He can also pick up some of the fundamentals of the game by himself. It will become apparent in time whether the boy or girl is *really* interested in golf and just how intent he or she is on becoming proficient in the game. If the desire is evident, then the schooling can start.

With adults, I believe it is desirable to start instruction immediately. It is much more difficult for adults to break bad swinging habits than it is for youngsters. If a fault is allowed to go uncorrected long enough in the swing of an adult, he must first break the bad habit, and then start from scratch to swing correctly.

Whether an adult takes up golf for exercise, social contacts, or business reasons, he should have sufficient motivation to develop a fair degree of skill at the game. However, it is the person who starts to play golf out of a keen interest in the game who will, in most cases, achieve the greatest skill.

Observation and Mimicking

The touring professionals who compete in tournaments and give exhibitions and demonstrations throughout the country make a very important contribution to good golfing form by providing models to be copied by others of lesser ability and accomplishment. To the thousands of spectators who observe them in action, they furnish a mental image or picture of a good golf swing. V irtually every human has the ability to mimic (if not to copy exactly) what he sees or hears. This allows him to benefit in his quest for golf learning by watching these top professionals who are the best possible models.

Today the men and women playing professionals make it a point to stage clinics wherever they appear in tournaments. These are for the benefit of all people interested in improving their golfing technique. In addition to demonstraitng proper form they answer questions raised by the onlookers. Their great wealth of "know-how" thus becomes available to anyone who wishes to draw from it.

3

The Grip and Stance

THE GRIP IS THE MOST IMPORTANT FACTOR IN A GOLF SWING. IF IT is not proper at all times, it is impossible to hit the ball as it should be hit. The hands are the No. 1 agent in the CONTROL of the clubhead, and control can hardly be overemphasized. Because the hands have a tendency to work themselves out of adjustment, it is essential that you check your grip constantly once you have learned the proper way to grip the club.

FEEL and TOUCH are also of utmost importance in swinging a golf club well. These senses must be developed to a high degree if anyone's golfing attainments are to be above ordinary. I heard one of America's foremost golfers say on the day of the closing round of a tournament, "My hands feel 'thin' today. I believe that I am going to play well." What he meant was that his hands felt keen or sensitive. Incidentally, he played well enough to win the championship.

Strength in the hands is not alone enough to insure proper hand action. *Feel* and *finesse* must also be present. When these qualities are combined with strength, then maximum results may be obtained from the hands as they play their part in the golf swing. Many golfers, including myself, use some form of hand exercise to keep their hands in condition. Let me caution that this can be overdone, leading to tired, sore muscles.

Sore Hands

Sore hands may result either from gripping the club too tightly, or else not tightly enough. Other causes are the tenderness that results from a layoff, and hands that work against each other because of improper relationship with one another on the club shaft.

Hand soreness may also result from clubs whose grips are not suited to the individual. This is one of the dangers in the practice of "handing down" clubs. If the grip is too large or too small, it is impossible for the hands to assume the proper grip on the club. The average woman using a club intended for a man is apt to develop sore hands because chances are that the weight is too great for her to handle, and the grip is too large.

The proper grip on the proper club shaft will do much to reduce the danger of sore hands.

Types of Grip

There are three basic types of grip: (1) The good old-fashioned baseball grip. (2) The interlocking grip which was more commonly used several years ago. (3) The Harry Vardon or overlapping grip in vogue today. This latter is the one we will consider. I prefer it because I believe that it is best-suited to the average player.

Placing Hands on the Club

When I first received instruction in placing my hands on the club I was told to stand erect, then bend slightly from the waist and hips, letting my hands hang in a natural position. The next step was to bring them forward toward the center of my body.

LEFT HAND — I place my left hand on the club shaft as shown in Illustration 1, with the "V" formed by my thumb and forefinger pointing up to my right shoulder. The thumb is about halfway between the top and the right side of the shaft (see Illustration 1).

My grip is very firm with my little finger and the two adjoining fingers, but is not tense to the extent of tightening the muscles in my left forearm.

Illustration 2 merely shows the position of the club shaft in my hand. Note that the shaft is not in the palm of my hand, but rather lies at an angle starting at the second joint of my forefinger and extending up across the base of my little finger. I always make certain that my left hand is *entirely* on the shaft of the club. In other words, it is in such position that a part of the shaft extends beyond the heel of my left hand. This is to insure complete control.

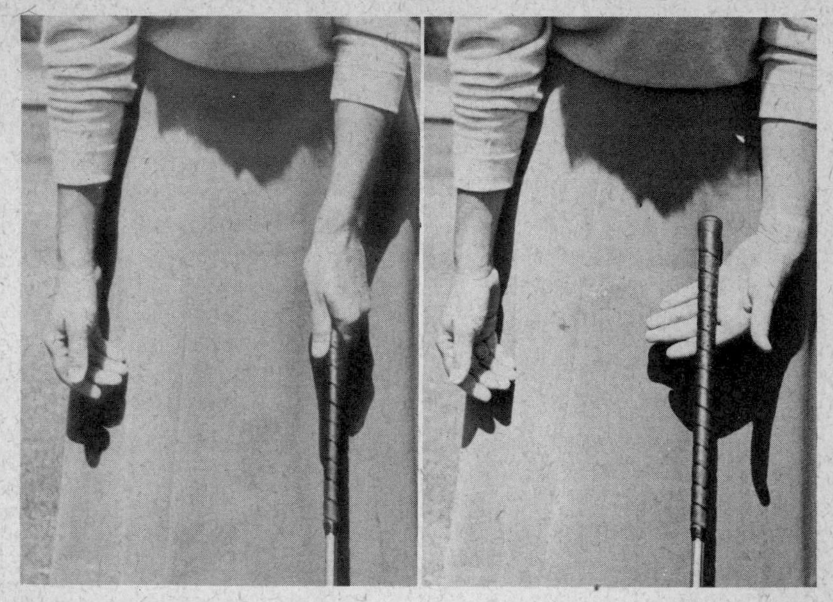

Illustration 1

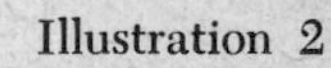

Illustration 2

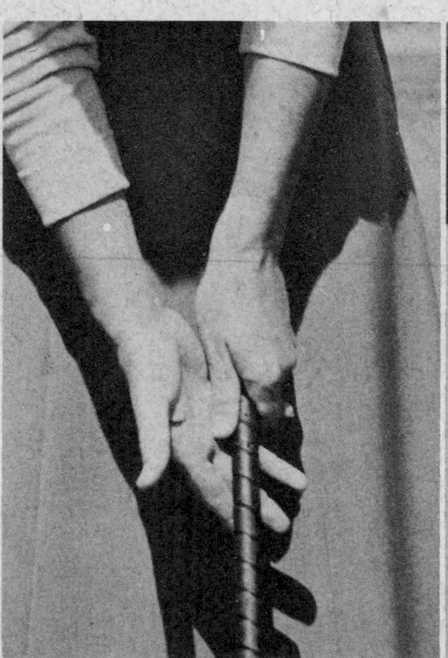

Illustration 3

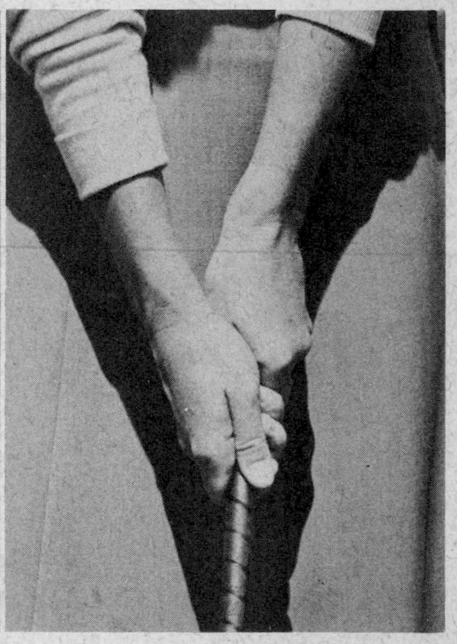

Illustration 4

Precautions: Don't let the grip change to the extent that you are using either a palm grip or a finger grip.

Don't let the shaft work down in your hands so that your left hand is partially off the top of the shaft. Check yourself frequently to make sure that your left hand is not working itself over around to the right on the shaft, or to the left and under the shaft. Either fault is certain to lessen your "feel" with the club. Either will radically affect your accuracy in hitting the ball.

RIGHT HAND – I place my right hand on the club shaft much as though I were going to "shake hands" with it. The little finger of my right hand overlaps between the knuckles of middle finger and the forefinger of my left hand.

The thumb of my left hand fits into the crease or "pocket" formed by the bending of the palm of my right hand around the club shaft (see Illustration 3 for proper placing of right hand).

Here again the thumb is *not* placed directly on the top of the shaft, but extends slightly across the shaft at an angle as shown in Illustration 4. The purpose of this is to avoid the tension that results from placing the thumb straight down the top of the shaft. Anything that creates tension in any phase of the golf swing is undesirable.

The "V" formed by the thumb and the forefinger of the right hand should correspond to or be at the same angle as the "V" formed by the same digits of the left hand (see Illustration 4).

Precautions: Carefully check yourself here again to make sure that your right hand does not work up and over the club shaft, or down and under the shaft. All too frequently, there is a tendency to hit with the right hand, and any deviations from the proper position greatly accentuate any fault in the flight of the ball.

Coordination of Hands

The hands should work together as a unit. You can see by a study of Illustration 5 that the fingers are as close together as they can comfortably be (without being tight). The hands are compactly

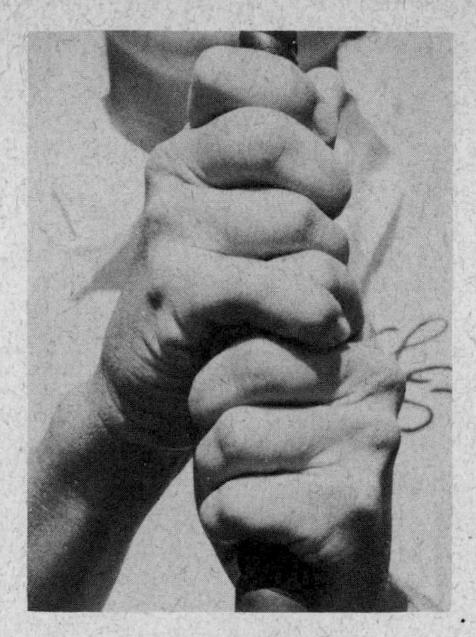

Illustration 5

together to insure control of the club which is impossible if the fingers or hands (or both) are spread.

Position at the Ball

In Illustration 6 I am standing up to the ball with a No. 5 iron. This iron was selected because it is a "medium" iron, halfway between a "long" iron (No. 2) and a "short" iron (No. 9).

The important points to observe in connection with position at the ball are the following (as shown in Illustration 6):

1. My arms and hands are hanging in a normal, comfortable position. In this position they will freely clear by body as they go through the swinging motion.

2. I am bending forward slightly from the hips but definitely NOT STOOPING. I am *balanced comfortably.*

3. My weight is evenly distributed between the balls and the heels of my feet, and between my right and left feet.

4. The distance I stand away from the ball is determined by the length of the club shaft. The sole of the club is flush with the ground.

Illustration 6

5. My knees are slightly flexed or bent to help me avoid stiffness and tension.

Because the length of the club will determine your proximity to the ball, it is *very* important that you have clubs whose degree of uprightness (the angle formed by the blade and the shaft), and length are best suited to you. A person's height is the most important determining factor in making this choice. Any qualified authority can help you make the correct choice of clubs.

The most important precaution to observe is to avoid *reaching* for the ball. This is a very common fault. In reaching for the ball you destroy balance, comfort, and the relaxed feeling so important to a good golf swing. The more one reaches for the ball, the greater is the tendency to flatten the arc and follow the general pattern of a baseball swing.

4

Playing the Drive

THE DRIVE, MORE THAN ANY OTHER SHOT IN GOLF, IS THE ONE THAT seems to invite everyone to "knock the cover" off the ball. The objective *should* be to get good, average distance that is within one's own physical capabilities, while striving for accuracy. The longest hitters off the tee are not necessarily the best scorers, particularly when they are "powering the ball" to the extent that they are wild in their direction.

Address

In Illustration 7 I am addressing the ball for a tee shot. The ball is played slightly forward of center of my stance. I generally use a square (see Illustration 8a) to slightly closed stance (see Illustration 8c). Note the straight line formed between my left shoulder and the ball by my left side. My weight is equally distributed between my right and left feet, and between the toes and heels of both feet. My knees are slightly flexed for comfort and freedom of movement.

Start of the Backswing

I have a mannerism with my hands and wrists just before the start of the backswing that is designed to break tension and pave the way for a smooth-flowing, rhythmic backswing. What I do is carry my hands forward in unison just an inch or two while the clubhead remains stationary. My right knee flexes slightly at the same time. The return of my hands and knees to their original position at the address of the ball develops in a continuous motion into the backswing. This "forward press" as it is known is essential

Illustration 7

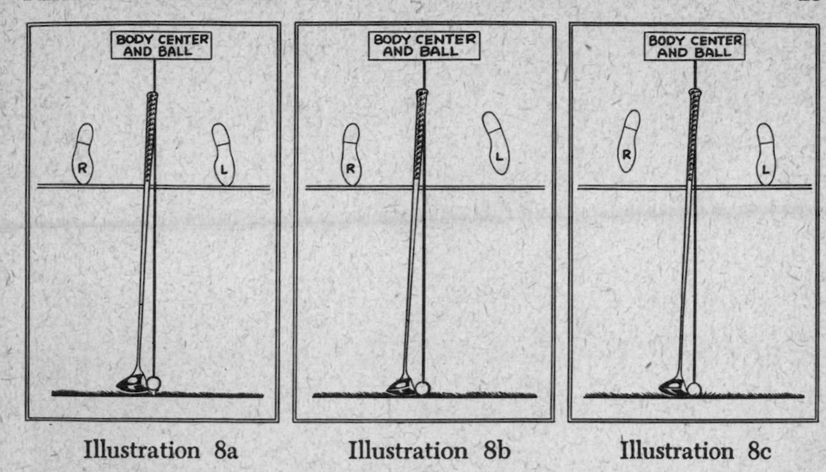

Illustration 8a Illustration 8b Illustration 8c

to avoid the jerking motion that is apt to result from a cold, rigid start on the backswing.

You will note in Illustration 9 that I have started my backswing. The clubface is still square to the ball and is being pushed back in a low trajectory. My weight is just beginning to go over from my left to my right foot. You can see that the clubhead has not been "picked up" by my right hand, for my left arm and the shaft still form a straight line. My hands are working together, but I have the feeling that my left hand is *pushing* the club back away from the ball. My right hand is just "riding" at this point.

Every part of my body is working as a unit. Observe that the left knee is beginning to flex to accommodate the turn of the hips and the shoulders which starts at this point. My right leg is bracing (not becoming rigid) so that it can bear the weight of my body as the transfer to the right side takes place. This transfer continues during the backswing.

Illustration 10. At this point in the backswing the wrists are just beginning to "cock." This is not a conscious effort. It is caused by the upward pull resulting from the momentum of the clubhead. At this point, as well as all others in the backswing, the motion is a rhythmic, graceful one. During the course of the backswing there should be no thought of how you are going to "murder" the ball when you finally get back to it. The best insurance for a well-hit ball is a backswing that puts you in position to have full control of the downswing and thus insure maximum hitting efficiency.

Illustration 9

Illustration 10

The turn of my hips and shoulders continues, as does the transfer of weight from my left to right side. While my head is turning with the shoulders as it must to avoid rigidity and tenseness, it remains in its original position and my eyes are fixed on the spot on the ball I expect to hit.

My left arm remains straight and firm, but not tense. My right arm is breaking at the elbow but remaining comparatively close to my body.

As shown in Illustration 11 my weight is pronouncedly over on my right side, and the inside of my left foot is now carrying what weight remains on my left side, and my left knee continues to give with the turn of my hips and shoulders. My head is still turning, but remains in its original position and my eyes are fixed on the ball.

Note particularly that my left arm is still straight. The momentum of the clubhead continues to carry the clubhead back into more of a cocked position.

Top of the Backswing

In Illustration 12 I have arrived at the top of my backswing. In so doing I have set the pattern for my downswing into the ball. It is the opinion of every golf authority that if the backswing is properly executed, it is virtually impossible to hit the ball poorly. About the only thing that could cause you to do so, if you have gotten to the top of your backswing correctly, is for your footing to give way.

Remember this: the ills that throw a golf swing out of kilter develop in the course of the backswing. It is virtually impossible to cure them by remedies in the downswing. If the backswing is faulty, it is impossible to hit the ball consistently straight and far. Any good results obtained under these circumstances are purely accidental.

My back is now turned toward my objective. The turn of my shoulders has pulled my head seemingly out of position. Such is not the case. It has had to turn on its own axis with the turning of my shoulders, but out of the corner of my left eye, I can still see the point on the ball at which I am aiming.

Many golfers have entirely the wrong notion of what the head is supposed to do. They have been warned: "Keep your head

Illustration 11

Illustration 12

down." "Keep your eye on the ball." "Don't move your head." This leads them to keep it in a fixed position which is completely unnatural. It is humanly impossible to turn your shoulders into the position in which you observe them in Illustration 12, and still keep your face pointed straight down at the ground. In doing this, you would disastrously restrict the backswing. However, your eyes should still be on the ball.

It is TRUE that you must *not* MOVE the head. It is UNTRUE you must not TURN it. It helps you to understand the head in relation to the rest of the golf swing if you think of it as the hub around which revolves the spokes (which are in this case the arms). If the clubhead is to travel in the desired trajectory the head must not deviate from its original relationship to the ball.

Observe that my left arm remains straight and firm. This is an important factor in keeping the clubhead in the desired downward trajectory, and in bringing it into the ball SQUARELY. If the left arm bends or collapses, the clubhead automatically deviates from its intended course. When this happens a missed or badly-hit shot is sure to result.

Note that my hands are still firmly on the clubshaft (see insert in Illustration 12) and in full control of the club. Note particularly that my right hand is under the shaft. In this position the hands are set to deliver the clubhead into the ball with the greatest possible efficiency.

The transfer of my weight to the right foot is now complete as seen in Illustration 12. My left foot serves merely as a balancing point at this stage. I am well balanced and ready for the downswing.

Start of the Downswing

At the start of the downswing my sensation is that of *pulling* the clubhead with my *left hand* back to the ball in the same arc as that described by the clubhead during the backswing. The position of my hands and wrists in relation to my arms is practically the same as it was at the top of my backswing.

The Downswing

The transfer of weight from my right to left side starts at the

Illustration 13

Illustration 14

Illustration 15

same moment my arms and hands begin their downward course. It is well under way at the point seen in Illustration 13. My body has already completed much of the uncoiling process. However, let me precaution you against making a conscious effort to rush the turning of the hips. This should be part of a coordinated motion in which the hands, wrists, arms, shoulders, hips, legs, and feet work together to get the clubhead back to the ball with the face square to the intended line of flight, and with a maximum of controlled velocity.

In this position my hands lead the clubhead. My wrists have not yet begun to start their "lash" at the ball, and my weight is almost evenly distributed between my right and left feet at this point. My left arm remains an accurate guide to the clubhead in describing its intended arc, because it is still straight.

The most important point to note in Illustration 14 is that my hands are in position to throw their full power behind the clubhead as it nears the "hitting area" which with me is approximately the final foot and a half before the impact of the clubhead with the ball.

My weight is now over on my left side, as you can see in Illustration 14 from the fact that my right heel is well off the ground. My head has now followed the turn of my shoulders back into approximately the same position as at the address. My left leg has become the foundation of my left side which is firm as it must be to permit me to lash at the ball with full power and still remain completely in balance. Note in Illustration 14 that my right elbow is hugging my right side, without being restricted by it.

Impact with Ball

As seen in Illustration 15 the ball has just been sent on its way by the clubhead. It is the only shot in which you normally hit the ball on the upswing.

I have the feeling that I have "slapped" the ball off the tee with the back of my left hand. Note that the palm of my right hand is facing my objective. This is always evidence that the clubhead has met the ball squarely — that is if you have taken the proper grip and stance at the outset.

My clubhead is following the flight of the ball, but will soon start to turn upward and inside the line of flight. My weight has

Illustration 16

transferred well over on to my left foot. Because I have not tried to slug at the ball or "kill" it I am in good balance.

After contact with the ball the essential points to note are:

(1) That my head turns to follow the flight of the ball. This is caused by the natural pull of the shoulders as they rotate to a full finish.

(2) My hands are well up, slightly above the top of my head. This is a normal consequence of a correct swing, and shouldn't be forced. There is no tendency to lose control of the club, even at this point.

(3) My weight is now completely over on my left foot, but there has been no tendency to fall away from the ball and I am still well balanced.

As seen in Illustration 16, my shoulders and hips have completed a full turn from their position at the top of the backswing (see Illustration 12). Because my head has followed the turn of my shoulders, as it must to avoid tension and a conflict in muscular function, my eyes are now directed toward my objective.

Observe the straight line running from my left ankle to my right shoulder, indicating that I am still well-balanced. Even though the finish has been full, my hands are still in control of the club.

5

Playing the Fairway Wood

THE SWING EMPLOYED IN PLAYING A FAIRWAY WOOD IS IDENTICAL TO that with which the tee shot is hit. Both shots are played well forward of the center of the stance.

Because the shaft of the spoon is a trifle shorter than that on the driver, I am standing a little closer to the ball, relaxed, but firm throughout (see Illustration 17).

Many people stand up to this shot with misgiving, for they lack faith in the ability of the clubhead to get the ball off the ground. Today's golf clubs are made to exacting standards. The technicians who design and build them make sure that the loft on the face of the club is sufficient to insure their doing their work properly.

Notice in Illustration 17 that my hands are in the same relationship to the ball as they would be were they holding a pendulum which was intended to strike the ball at the exact bottom of its arc. In this case the club is the pendulum. My hands are the axis from which it swings.

Because the swing for the shot under consideration here is identical to that employed in hitting a tee shot, I will touch on only the most important points in connection with each of the eight Illustrations that follow.

In Illustration 18 note that the clubhead is being *pushed* back from the ball with the left hand and side. All components of the swing are in full harmony. The trajectory is low and straight back from the ball to this point.

Illustration 19 catches the hands just about waist height – the point in the backswing where they start the cocking motion.

I have not quite arrived at the top of my backswing at the instant shown in Illustration 20. I call your attention to the firmness of

Illustration 17

Illustration 18

Illustration 19

Illustration 20

Illustration 21

Illustration 22

Illustration 23

Illustration 24

the left arm and the full control of the club by both hands.

In Illustration 21 we see the hands well-started on their downward course. They appear to be leading the club at this point. This is because the power of the hands and wrists is being held in reserve for the final lash at the ball.

Note in Illustration 22 how I am practically square to the ball just before the moment of impact. Hands and wrists are now at the height of exertion of their power.

Because the club shaft and my left arm form a perfect pendulum at this point, it is certain that the clubhead will meet the ball on the proper plane when the shoulder remains in position. As my hands have returned to the exact position in which I placed them at the address, the clubhead *must* meet the ball squarely. In other words, In other words, all the criteria of a well hit shot are present.

The principals of the finish of the swing as portrayed Illustrations 23 and 24 are identical to those covered in the discussion of the finish in playing the drive.

6

Playing the Irons

I AM FREQUENTLY ASKED, "HOW DO YOU DECIDE BETWEEN A LONG IRON such as a No. 2 or No. 3 iron and a No. 4 wood in playing a shot from the fairway?"

The lie of the ball has something to do with my choice. Personally if I have a close or heavy lie (one in which the ball is not sitting up cleanly on the turf) I prefer to use a No. 4 wood. First of all, the wood is heavier and will get through grass or clover in front of the ball more easily than the blade of an iron. And secondly, the face of the wood is not as apt to be turned off line as is the blade of an iron.

Playing conditions are also a determining factor. Everything being equal, the No. 4 wood will provide about the same distance as a No. 2 iron. However, when long carry is desirable, I will use a No. 4 wood. It is my choice when the turf is wet and heavy. When I can anticipate a long roll on the ball I will use a No. 2 iron.

Wind is a rather important consideration. When playing into a strong wind I choose a No. 2 iron in preference to a No. 4 wood because the flight of the ball is lower with the iron and therefore the ball is not as apt to be blown off its course.

Many golfers fear a No. 2 iron because the blade appears to have a very slight loft. This belief leads them to try to "help" or force the ball up into the air by making adjustments in the course of their swing. The results are usually disastrous. Again I say that all good clubs today are so well engineered and designed that you needn't worry about their ability to produce the results for which they are intended.

No Basic Difference in Swings

All too many golfers are obsessed with the erroneous idea that there is a basic difference between the swing employed in playing an iron shot and the swing for a wood shot. This is not true. In fact, it has been my observation that many of the difficulties encountered by golfers having trouble in hitting their iron shots is that they have the notion that they must bring the clubhead into the ball in a sharper downward course. This is the result of words they have heard about "striking the ball a descending blow." Consequently you can observe the so-called "hackers" on virtually any course bringing the clubhead down with much the same stroke they would use in swinging an axe.

I repeat: (1) That development of a MENTAL PICTURE is essential to playing good golf. (2) Golf should be played by FEEL.

It is true that the clubhead is actually descending at the point of impact in any iron shot. However, it is imperative that we *feel* that we are *swinging through* the ball toward the objective, rather than with a sharply descending blow. It helps if you get the feeling that you are trying to sweep the clubhead through the ball with the left hand rather than concentrating intently on the mere act of picking the ball off the turf. Or expressed another way, don't try to "chop" or lift the ball off the turf.

We will find as we continue the study of the shorter irons, that our swing must become more upright, but this is because as the number of the iron increases, the shaft becomes shorter. Obviously the radius of the arc described by the clubhead must decrease.

Playing the Long Iron

Note in Illustration 25 that at the address of the ball, it is opposite a point approximately two inches inside my left heel. My stance is square and my weight is equally distributed on both feet. My hands are slightly ahead of the ball, and a little forward of the center of my body. I am standing fairly erect, but my hands are hanging in a normal position and close to my body.

As shown in Illustration 26 I am starting the clubhead back, away from the ball. Note particularly the low trajectory of the clubhead which is still moving *straight back* from the ball. Everything is working together. *There is no emphasis on any one component of*

Illustration 25

Illustration 26

Illustration 27

Illustration 28

the body. The transfer of weight has already proceeded to the extent that it is well over on my right foot. My left knee is flexing slightly. My shoulders have already begun to turn with my hips, and my head is being pulled around by the shoulders.

While the clubhead, as shown in Illustration 27, is now well into its upward arc, it is rising in a full, free-swinging, rhythmic motion, and the left hand is still in control. At no time is there any attempt by the right hand to *pick* it up. At the stage of the swing in Illustration 28, I have not quite reached the top of the backswing, and my wrists have not cocked to the full extent as at the top of the backswing. Note that the coiling process of the body is still in progress.

When I arrive at the top of my full backswing, the timing has been such that my *entire* body is ready to initiate the downswing with the hands leading the way. There has been no lag by hands, wrists, arms, shoulders, hips, legs, or feet. They all arrived together at the point of readiness for the downswing.

The shaft of the club is parallel to the ground. My left arm is comfortably extended at this point. This is the criterion of the extent to which the backswing should extend. If I were to let the clubhead drop beyond the point it has reached at the top of my backswing, it could happen only through a collapse of my left arm, wrists, or hands. As it is, my hands are fully in control of the club and my wrists are firm.

Avoiding Flat Swing

As you can see, my hands are higher than the top of my head. This is possible only when you start the clubhead back in a low trajectory *straight* away from the ball, with the back of your left hand toward your objective. If you will observe this rule, you will avoid the error of rolling your hands over or under at the beginning of the backswing. In other words, try to swing arms, wrists, hands, and clubhead straight back just as far as you can without moving your head out of position and then upward in a natural, swinging motion, rather than in a circular motion revolving around the body. When that error is committed, the clubhead comes back sharply inside the line of flight, leading to what is known as a "flat swing," or "roundhouse swing."

Let me urge you to carry in your own mind a mental image of the position you want to attain at the top of your backswing. If you will do this, and then try to match it, chances are that with a little practice you will execute your backswing properly. This is the simplest approach to developing a good golf swing. It is much more effective than trying to think of the backswing as a series of motions.

Important! Having a clear mental picture of what you are trying to do at all times is the most effective way I know for learning and retaining a mechanically-sound golf swing.

Having arrived properly at the top of my backswing, I needn't be concerned over what will take place in the course of my downswing. I am completely in control. I have established the rhythm and the pattern on the way up that I will automatically duplicate on the way down.

The main difference is in the expenditure of energy just before clubhead contact with the ball. In Illustration 29 you see me turning loose this energy that was generated in the course of the backswing. The clubhead is about to enter the hitting area, and at

Illustration 29 Illustration 30

this point, the right hand throws its full power behind the momentum of the clubhead. It is the precision and coordination with which this stored-up energy is applied that will in a large measure determine the accuracy and distance attained in the shot.

By the time the clubhead reaches the point shown in Illustration 30, the transfer of weight from the right to left side is nearing completion.

Note in Illustration No. 30 that the club is continuing toward its objective on exactly the same trajectory in which it was pushed away from the ball at the start of the backswing. Reversing the procedure of the backswing, the natural turning of the body will bring the clubhead inside the line of flight and upward. This correct follow-through is the natural consequence of a well-executed backswing. There should be no forcing or deliberate attempt to steer or maneuver the hands. Do let me caution you *not to quit* at this point. The velocity and momentum of the clubhead should bring you naturally to a full and proper finish.

The transfer of my weight to the left side is complete at the stage shown in Illustration 31. Note that even at this point, my momentum

Illustration 31

Illustration 32

Illustration 33 Illustration 34

is more toward the objective than to the left of the line of flight (for the right-handed golfers).

I believe that the greatest single factor in the remarkable increase in accuracy and consistency among good golfers in the past 15 years has been the wide acceptance of this principle: Keep the clubhead on the line of flight (with the back of the left hand square to the objective) for the greatest possible distance back away from the ball and then on through after impact. By "greatest possible distance" is meant to the extent that the swinging motion does not become unnatural or strained. This principle will increase the likelihood of the clubface being square to the line of flight at the point of impact with the ball.

There is not even the slightest tendency for my hands to lose control of the club and my wrists are still firm. The shaft of my No. 2 iron is pointing directly at my objective.

In Illustration 32 the follow through is complete. The momentum generated in the downswing was sufficient to carry club and hands around to this position without any conscious effort. It is a completely natural finish. At this point my body has completed a full turn and I am facing squarely toward my objective. Because there has been no attempt to "murder the ball" I am perfectly balanced.

Playing the Medium Iron

The basic differences between the stance for a long iron shot and the stance for a medium iron shot (as demonstrated in Ilustration 33) are as follows:

1. The ball is now at a point exactly opposite the center of my stance. For the long iron it was slightly forward of center.
2. My stance is slightly open (see Illustration 8b). In playing the long iron my stance was square (Illustration 8a).
3. I am standing closer to the ball because the shaft is shorter. To compensate for the shorter shaft I must bend a little more at the waist. Please do not confuse "bend" with "lean."

Because I will employ full power in hitting this shot, the width of my base remains the same. By this I mean that the distance between my feet is still the same as the width of my shoulders (as it was for the woods and the long irons). The principle of the swing I use in playing a medium iron is exactly the same as that observed in playing a long iron, so we will not repeat the basic considerations discussed previously.

In Illustration 34 note that even when using a *medium* iron, I observe the same rule – pushing the clubhead back low and straight. As this movement continues, the straight line formed by my left arm and the club shaft seen in Illustration 35 disappears, because the process of "cocking" my wrists gets well under way. Bear in mind very clearly that this "cocking" action is not a quick or jerky motion in which you suddenly flip the hands and clubhead upward. It conforms to the smooth, continuous, rhythmic tempo of the backswing.

Note in Illustration 35 that my head is turning with the pull of my shoulders, but you may be sure that my eyes are very definitely fixed at the point on the ball I intend to meet with the club face. Make no effort to retard this turning of your head. Turning is a fault only when it is accompanied by *moving* or shifting. If you will closely observe the position of my head in relation to the tree in the background, you will see that it has *not moved,* though it has turned.

Illustration 35 Illustration 36

While the transfer of weight from the left to the right side is virtually complete, there has been absolutely *no swaying.* I find that some golfers who are having swing trouble think that they are turning or pivoting when they are *actually* swaying and shifting. It goes without saying that if you shift your body away from its original relationship to the ball, your chances of hitting the ball are very slim, even if you try to sway back into balance. This motion will throw your timing and coordination completely off, and will, of course, destroy the constant arc in which your clubhead must travel if it is to meet the ball squarely and well-timed.

In Illustration 36, I have arrived at the top of my backswing and am now ready to start the clubhead on its downward course. My balance is good for I have made no attempt to get ready to "murder the ball."

There is just a slight hesitation on my part at this point, but it is scarcely visible to the observer. It is the best way I know to make sure that you do not start your downswing before completing your backswing. This is a common error, particularly in those golfers who are intent on "pouring everything they have" into hitting the ball. Do not pause more than momentarily at the top, for if you do you will break the rhythm of your swing. It shouldn't be a conscious or deliberate effort. When your sense of timing is functioning properly, a pause of the right length will automatically develop.

When I am at the top of my backswing and ready to return the clubhead to the ball, the only thought of which I am conscious is to start the clubhead down with my hands. I am not concerned with the physical act of hitting the ball. In other words, I am not thinking about what my left hip may be doing, what my left arm is going to do, or the position of my hands in relationship to the club face.

If I have taken a good stance, assumed the proper grip on the club and observed the other basic rules for getting ready to hit the ball, there is no need to think about what is happening and what is going to happen. Once you have grasped the proper fundamentals of the swing and have practiced what you have learned, it becomes "second nature" to swing correctly. You will have to think of the components of your swing only when something is wrong. The thing to do then, rather than concern yourself with self-analysis, is to get competent instruction. I have seen a minor fault that was bothering a good golfer ironed out in 30 seconds by a simple suggestion from a qualified authority. Often if you try to cure your own golfing ills you are apt to develop others because of improper analysis of the true source of the trouble.

From the point at which the club is seen in Illustration 37 on in to the ball, there isn't much that can happen to cause you to miss the shot – IF your backswing has been proper.

The main point to be noticed in Illustration 38 is the "readiness" of the hands to go to work in propelling the clubhead into the ball with maximum velocity.

As shown in Illustration 39, the clubhead has just sent the ball on its way. Despite the weight transfer over to my left foot, which is well toward completion at this point, I have not in any way swayed off balance and am still centered on the spot from which the ball was played. The face of my club is still perfectly square to the line of flight, as is the back of my left hand.

Even at the next stage of the swing I have not swayed at all. My eyes follow the flight of the ball, and my head has merely *turned* in its original position.

Illustration 37

Illustration 38

Illustration 39

Illustration 40

A combination of great clubhead speed through the ball and natural unrestricted body motion has made it possible for the clubhead to come around to the finish point shown in Illustration 40. I want particularly to point out that I have in no way extended or forced myself to arrive at this position. My hands are just as firmly in control of the club as they were at any stage of the swing (see insert in Illustration 40 for a close up) though of course they have long since ceased to apply any force to the club.

Playing the Short Iron

The basic considerations to keep in mind when studying the technique of playing a short iron are the following:

1. This is a *full* shot.
2. An open stance is employed (see Illustration 8b). The width of the stance is still equal to that of the shoulders.
3. I play the ball off the center of my stance. The open stance creates the illusion that the ball is being played from a point back of center of my stance.
4. The arc describe by the clubhead on the backswing is more upright because of the shorter club shaft.
5. *Accuracy,* not distance, is the principal objective in playing this club.
6. That the lofted club face will get the ball up in the air does not necessarily mean that the ball will stop suddenly when it lands. Only when the ball is struck firmly with a sharply-descending blow will the backspin necessary for a quick stop result.

Because the person using a short iron (Nos. 7, 8, or 9) is primarily concerned with *accuracy* or hitting the ball up to the pin, the tendency is to try and "steer" or "guide" the ball. This is bad. This thinking shouldn't even enter in. Develop enough confidence in your ability to line yourself up with your objective so that you don't even give it a second thought.

A prevalent misconception is that the higher the flight of the ball, the more quickly will it stop. This causes some golfers to try to help the ball into the air. The usual consequence is a scuffed or half-topped shot.

Another common difficulty in playing a short iron stems from the natural desire, when accuracy is uppermost in the mind, to "peek" or to look up suddenly at the objective rather than to concentrate on striking the ball precisely at the intended spot. Anyone who has played golf knows the consequences of this mistake. Almost anything in the "dubbed" category may result.

Illustration 41 gives the impression that I am leaning back on my right foot at the address of the shot with a short iron. This is an illusion. Actually the weight is evenly distributed between both feet, just as it is for all other shots. Without this distribution there cannot be the proper balance so essential to the proper execution of all golf shots. The shaft of the short irons is even shorter than those of the medium irons. This means that I must bend a little more at the waist to place my hands on the club properly.

As you will note in Illustration 42 the clubhead is pushed back, away from the ball, just as in playing the shots we have previously considered. It is at the point shown that the blade of the club starts to open up a little because of the revolving motion of the body. I particularly call your attention to the fact that I am not "picking the club up." Here again the arc will be just as full as can possibly be described with a club of this length. Note the cocking action beginning in my wrists.

The position shown in Illustration 43 is the exact top of my backswing. Because the radius of the arc that can be described with this short club is less than that described by a club with a longer shoft, the momentum of the clubhead is not as great. Consequently, it is not carried naturally as far back as would be a club of greater length when the same amount of force is applied.

As shown in Illustration 44, my hands are leading the clubhead down. There has been no attempt to unleash their power. The left hand is in control. My weight is about evenly distributed.

At the stage of the downswing exhibited in Illustration 45 my hands are ready to unleash their full power. The right hand has *followed* the left hand down to this point, but will in an instant throw its full force into swinging the clubhead at the ball.

Note in Illustration 46 how the back of my left hand is still squarely toward my objective as the ball starts on its way.

For the benefit of those harboring the misconception that you must cut down through the turf and take a big divot to get the ball into the air I call your attention to the fact that I have scarcely

Illustration 41

Illustration 42

Illustration 43

Illustration 44

Illustration 45 Illustration 46

Illustration 47 Illustration 48

disturbed the turf with the blade of the club. I have merely cut through the base of the grass with the sole of the club, striking the ball and the turf at the same moment. This imparts a pronounced backspin to the ball. The bottom of my arc is just slightly forward of the ball. Note the pendulum-like action of the arms and the club in Illustration 46.

One of the most important precautions that comes to my mind in connection with the playing of this shot is to not permit the clubhead to be slowed or turned in your hands as the blade is caught by the grass through which it must pass. I find that many people have a tendency to flip the clubhead at the ball in playing a short iron, with the result that their grip on the club isn't firm enough and the wrists are loose. The results must suffer.

As you will see in studying Illustrations 47 and 48, this swing with the short iron must be carried through to completion in exactly the same manner as with any other club.

7

Pitching and Chipping

THE WOMAN GOLFER DOESN'T HAVE TO CONCEDE THE MAN A THING when the elements of strength and leverage are no longer a factor in swinging a club. It is my contention that the best of the women players can match the best of the men golfers from 125 yards out on in to the cup. Thus it behooves the woman with aspirations to become a low scorer to concentrate particularly on her short game.

One of the most important stroke-saving clubs in any golfer's bag is the wedge or double-service niblick. This club has a heavy flange or sole, and it very definitely has most of its "feel" in the head. Many of today's foremost golfers will tell you that it has been the perfecting of this club in recent years that has had much to do with the general improvement in scoring by the best amateurs and professionals.

Short Pitch with Wedge

The short pitch is most commonly used from within 50 yards or so of the pin in cases when you must get the ball up in the air and over obstacles (traps, etc.) between you and the green, or else onto an elevated green situated at a level above that from which the ball is being played, and yet make it stop abruptly.

It is the ideal shot in the above described situations when the distance from the edge of the green nearest you to the cup is very limited, for when properly executed with the wedge, the stroke imparts pronounced backspin which causes the ball to stop short on landing. Because the action of the ball after striking the turf can thus be restricted, it is known as a "control" shot.

This club is of particular importance to a woman, who because of lack of great hitting power or strength, often finds herself short of a par four hole after her second shot. Or, in extending herself in trying to get home in two shots, she may hit off line with the result that she is wide of the green. In these instances the wedge may be an invaluable stroke-saver. If you master its use, chances are you can put the ball up close to the hole for a single putt in a majority of instances. We find some of the more proficient girls today occasionally sinking one of these short pitches with a wedge. The frequency of occurrence is great enough so that we know it to be more skill than luck. The better players are not trying merely to get the ball up on to the green; they actually attempt to get the ball in the cup.

Because of the importance of acquiring finesse with this shot, we will study it from two angles so that you may better develop a complete mental image of the shot and more fully grasp all the details of playing it.

You can see in Illustration49 that my feet are not spaced quite as far apart as they were for the full shots. The hands and wrists, with

Illustration 49

Illustration 50

Illustration 51 Illustration 52

only very little help from the body, can provide all the power necessary. The reason for the abbreviated body turn in the execution of this shot is to avoid rigidity and to accommodate the swinging motion of the arms.

The ball is placed just slightly back of the center of the stance as you can see in Illustration 49. The stance is open as shown in Illustration 50. Also in this picture I am bending more from the waist than for any of the other shots considered earlier. The reason for this is that I am deliberately shortening my grip on the club, as is evident from the amount of the shaft that appears above my left hand.

I am standing well up to the ball because the nearer the center of gravity of your body to the ball, the more control you are apt to have in stroking it. Don't get the impression that because I am *bent* over more from the waist that I am *leaning* over. I am completely well-balanced.

In Illustrations 51 and 52, I am pushing the clubhead away from the ball. Even though the arms and wrists are doing the majority of the work, there is still no evidence that the clubhead is being picked

Illustration 53

Illustration 54

up by the right hand. This is still a continous, pendulum-like motion in which the fullest possible arc is described.

As you can see in Illustrations 53 and 54 the transfer of weight from the left to the right foot is much less pronounced than it was in executing the full shots. Even so, all working parts of the body are moving together in perfect coordination.

Though the clubhead is not swung as far back in the execution of this short pitch with the wedge as it is in the full shot with a short iron, my left arm is fully extended as you can see in Illustration 55 and 56, and my wrists are just as fully cocked.

The clubhead is starting its downward course into the ball. Illustration 57 shows the hands in position to release their power. In Illustration 58, they are in the act of releasing it.

Both Illustrations 59 and 60 show the clubhead and the ball just after the moment of impact. Note how sharply the ball is rising off the face of the club. It is very evident that my arms and the club shaft have swung in unison in the manner of a pendulum. My hips and shoulders were parallel to the line of flight at the time of impact. My weight is on my left foot, but not completely.

Illustration 55

Illustration 56

Illustration 57

Illustration 58

Illustration 59

Illustration 60

Illustration 61

Illustration 62

The momentum of the clubhead has been great enough so that it is not visibly or appreciably slowed down in cutting through the base of the grass through which it must pass at the bottom of its arc (just forward of the position of the ball). It is just as important for the clubhead to continue on through in a full, free-swinging motion in this shot as it is in a full shot. You can see in Illustrations 61 and 62 that the clubhead is continuing to a full finish just as it did in playing the full shots.

Pictured in Illustrations 63 and 64 is the finish of the short pitch shot with the wedge. Because the momentum added to a full shot by the action of the body is missing, and the arc described by the shorter club is smaller, the hands are not as high and the clubhead has not travelled as far as in the instance of a full shot. But let me impress on you that despite the lessening of the application of power to this shot, it has been executed in a firm and crisp manner.

Simple Chip Shot to Cup

Because of the very limited motion required by it, the simple

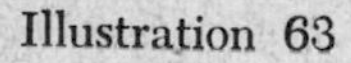

Illustration 63

Illustration 64

chip shot from the edge of the green is one of the easiest shots in golf to execute. Yet, probably because of lack of concentration and unwillingness to practice on the part of most people, it is one of the most troublesome in the common repertory of strokes.

The fundamentals involved in playing this shot properly are the following:

1. Be certain of your line. The face of the club blade must be perfectly square to the line on which you intend to hit the ball.

2. Weight is equally balanced on both feet, and is distributed evenly between the ball and heel of each foot.

3. Stance is open, and feet close together.

4. It is a hands-wrist-arms shot.

5. The ball is played from a point just slightly back of center of the stance (as shown in Illustration 65).

6. The clubhead is pushed straight back away from the ball on the line of flight, and follows through on the same line toward the hole after impact with the ball.

7. This is definitely a pendulum-like swing.

Illustration 65

Illustration 66

Illustration 67

Illustartion 68

Illustration 69

Illustration 70

Illustration 71 Illustration 72

I believe the most effective way to grasp the technique of this shot is to study carefully the series of Illustrations 66 through 72, and in this manner acquire a mental image to serve as a pattern to follow in playing this shot. Note particularly Illustration 68 which shows the full extent of the rise of my hands on the backswing, and Illustration 72 which shows the finish of the swing.

I usually call upon this shot when I am on the fringe of the green (from 1 to 20 feet off the green) and on level or only gently rolling terrain. This shot can be a great stroke-saver. It can be developed with only a reasonable amount of practice and application to the extent that the ball can be chipped up within easy putting distance of the hole in a large majority of attempts. The better professionals and amateurs expect to sink many of these shots for they are always "going for the hole" when they play it. Here again, it is a matter of touch and finesse. In playing this shot, I usually pick out a spot on the green where I want the ball to land, intending that it shall roll from this point to the cup.

8

Putting

THE THEORIES AND TECHNIQUES OF PUTTING THAT HAVE BEEN developed and expounded since the origin of the game of golf would fill many, many volumes. I doubt whether any two of the 20 best golfers in the world today have identical ideas on the subject. However, there are some basic principles which hold true for all players noted for their success in putting. They are:

1. A grip designed to enable the individual to keep the blade of the putter square to the line and on a low trajectory throughout its course. The grip must also facilitate the development of a fine sense of touch.
2. Confidence in that grip and the stroke. We frequently hear it said that putting is "all in the head."
3. Having the eyes directly above the ball to aid in keeping the blade of the club perfectly square to the line.
4. Intense concentration.
5. Firmness, but complete absence of muscular tension.
6. Balance in which the individual feels most comfortable. This may not necessarily mean equal distribution of weight between the feet

Observation of the series of putting photos Nos. 73 through 77 will give you a clear idea of the putting technique that I personally find most suitable. In No. 73 you see the position of the ball in relation to my feet. Note the proximity of my hands to my left leg. However they are not resting on my leg. My right elbow hugs my right hip, but doesn't press against it.

I have the feeling in stroking a putt that I am "tapping" the ball. By this I mean, I send it on its way with a sharp, crisp stroke that is fairly short as you will see in Illustration 74 (end of backstroke).

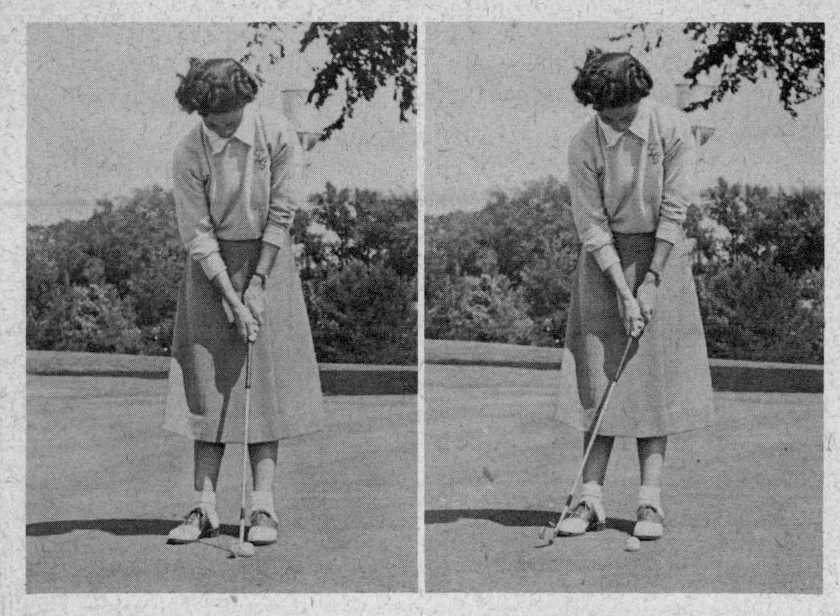

Illustration 73

Illustration 74

Illustration 75

Illustration 76

Illustration 77

Illustration 78

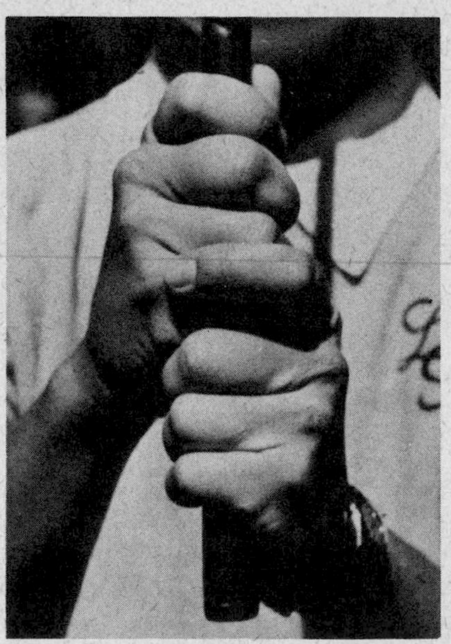

Illustration 79

The longer the putt, the more firmly I tap the ball.

I don't quit as soon as I strike the ball. Doing so would amount to "stabbing" it – one of the most common and disastrous putting faults. My blade follows through after the ball as you can see in Illustration 77. It does not move beyond the point shown in 77, but picture 78 is added as visual proof that this putt was accurately stroked.

Like most everyone else who has played golf extensively I experimented at length with my putting. Through this process of trial and error I arrived at the grip pictured in Illustration 79. I am gripping the club just as I would for any other shot, except that I have reversed the position of the little finger of my right hand. Rather than overlapping the forefinger of the left hand, it is placed on the club shaft, and the forefinger of the left hand is overlapping it. I do not say that this is the best putting grip for all people. I have simply found that it best suits my purposes in the respects mentioned in item No. 1 in the preceding list of principles.

The hands very definitely work together. The moment one hand overpowers the other in the course of a putting stroke, a loss of accuracy is bound to result.

Of paramount importance in assuring accuracy is the ability to line yourself up properly with the hole. Unless that is done the soundest putting stroke is of no avail. Once I have decided on the line of the putt, I focus my attention on the point of the ball I intend to strike. My eyes don't turn toward the hole again until the ball is well on its way. The ability to "see the line" and to "read the green" is something that must be cultivated through repetition and experience. Time spent in developing this ability is well spent. All too few people give adequate thought to this *very* important phase of putting.

The law of average in sinking putts is always in favor of the "bold" putter who gets the ball either in or past the cup. In other words, he always "gives it a chance." If you are timid and fall consistently short, you are ignoring simple percentages.

Too many golfers tend to blame their putting troubles on the putter rather than on themselves. Select a putter that seems to be best suited to you and has the best "feel." Then stay with it and do your best to develop confidence in it. No one lacking confidence can become a consistently good putter.

The fact that it is so important to have the blade of the putter square to the intended line of the putt seems to lead to a common misconception that the entire putting stroke must be exactly on this line. This is not true. If you continue to take the blade back straight beyond the point at which it would turn inside the line of flight with the natural swinging motion of your hands and wrists you are actually forcing it outside the line of flight. This is an unnatural motion and as such is undersirable.

The relaxation essential to good putting is evident in the accompanying series of pictures.

9

Getting Out of Trouble

Playing Long Iron From Rough

THE SWING EMPLOYED IN PLAYING A LONG IRON FROM THE ROUGH IS the same as that used in any other long iron shot. The fact that the ball rests in long grass creates a basic problem: How to get the ball into the air with minimum interference from the grass?

To achieve this the ball must be played slightly forward of center of the stance so that the face of the club will meet the ball on the upswing. It is in this fashion only that a woman can get distance on a shot played from the rough, for she lacks the power to get the blade of the club through the long grass surrounding the ball without interference. The overspin imparted to the ball by hitting it on the upswing adds to the roll of the ball once it strikes the turf. The result is added distance to the shot.

Because the ball is partially buried in the grass, it is a natural tendency on the part of most people learning golf to jump at the ball, or to try to "dig it out." The usual result is to stroke the ball deeper into trouble.

The best attitude toward the shot is to ignore the fact that the ball is partially obstructed. Just concentrate on swinging in the normal fashin. Have confidence that if you do your part properly the club will do its intended work.

I am playing the shot from the rough in Illustration 80 through 87 with a No. 4 iron. The basic principals involved are thoroughly covered in Chapter 6 on the Long Iron.

Trap Shot With Wedge

This is the shot that gives most golfers who are less than expert at

Illustration 80

Illustration 81

Illustration 82

Illustration 83

Illustration 84

Illustration 85

Illustration 86

Illustration 87

the game the well-known "quakes." Actually it is one of the easiest shots of all to play, once you know how to go about it.

Distance is not the important factor in playing this shot. It is usually a matter of getting the ball out of the sand trap and on to a nearby green.

The basic principles involved in this type of explosion shot are the following:

1. A *firm* foundation so that you will not slide around or move in the sand once you have started your stroke. Work your feet down into the sand until you feel that your footing is secure (see Illustration 99).

2. An open stance, with the ball opposite a point slightly back of the center of your stance (as shown in Illustration 99).

3. A firm but deliberate backswing.

4. Hit the sand before the ball. The greater the distance desired the closer to the ball you strike the sand. Be sure to concentrate on the point at which you want the clubhead to enter the sand. There is no hard and fast formula for the amount of sand to be taken. This must be determined by practice and experience. The

Illustration 88 Illustration 89

object is to get the ball up in the air.

5. Employ a full swing. It is essential that you don't allow the clubhead to be "killed" by the sand. It must carry on through to a full finish just as in any other swing.

6. FIRMNESS of hands, wrists, and arms.

You can't touch the sand with the club before swinging. It is contrary to the rules of golf to ground or "sole" your club in a hazard. As you can see in Illustration 88 (in which I am addressing the ball for a trap shot with the wedge), my clubhead is directly above the point at which I intend to hit. In other words, I am addressing a point or spot rather than the ball itself. The latter is the case in the normal fairway shots.

You can see my arm and the clubshaft starting back in a straight line (Illustration 89) which again means that I will describe the fullest possible arc with the clubhead. Contrary to the practice of some people, there is no extra play of the hands or the wrists. You can see in Illustration 90 that only the usual amount of cocking action is in progress as the clubhead nears the level of my hips in the course of my backswing.

Illustration 90 Illustration 91

Illustration 92 Illustration 93

It is evident in Illustration 91 that a full backswing is made in playing this shot.

In Illustration 92 the downswing is under way, but there is no attempt to get ready to "power" the ball. Note the firm left arm.

At the stage of the downswing shown in Illustration 93 full application of power by the hands is starting.

When I strike the ball, the firmness of my hands and wrists does not yield a bit to the drag of the sand as the clubhead passes through it. Thus I am able to achieve a full finish as seen in Illustrations 94-95.

Because there has been no attempt to "slug" the ball or "lunge" at it as is so often the case with the golfing neophyte, I am in good balance and complete control of the club at the very end of the swing.

As a final word of caution – don't feel that you have to "help" the ball up out of the trap. This is a common error. The wedge club used for this purpose is the culmination of many years of development in club manufacture. It is ideally suited to this job, which it will perform amazingly well if you will just swing it as you should.

Illustration 94

Illustration 95

The heavy flange on the wedge serves to prevent the blade of the club from cutting down into the sand, and produces an action similar to that of a flat stone skimming across the water.

You MUST develop confidence. There is nothing tricky at all about this shot. Most low-handicap players of today don't try to merely get the ball out of the sand and on to the green. They play for the cup. You will read during the progress of nearly any major tournament today of one of the stars sinking one or more wedge shots from traps. This isn't an accident at all. It is merely the result of application and practice, and the *confidence* that follows.

Playing From Trap For Distance

On the occasions in which I find myself in a shallow trap and a long ways from my destination, I will use a long iron once I have determined that the loft of the face is great enough so that the ball will clear the edge of the trap. I think of this shot just exactly as I would any other long iron shot and swing at the ball in the very same manner.

Illustration 96

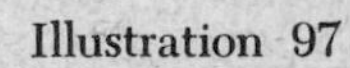

Illustration 97

Illustration 98

Illustration 99

The special considerations to be borne in mind are the following:

1. You cannot sole the club in the sand. See Illustration 96.

2. The feet must be "worked" down into the sand to assure a firm foundation.

3. The clubface must meet the ball and the sand at the same time.

4. More than ordinary determination to hit *through* the ball firmly so that the clubhead will not be retarted by the sand.

Here again there is no reason for fear or doubt as to your ability to hit the ball cleanly and effectively (see Illustrations 97-100).

You can see in Illustration 96 that I am playing the ball from slightly forward of the center of my stance.

Bearing the four points listed above in mind, the principles of the shot are the same as those discussed in Chapter 6 on the Long Irons.

Illustrations 101, 102, 103 make it evident that the sand through which the clubhead has passed has in no way prevented me from swinging through to a full firm finish.

Illustration 100 Illustration 101

Illustration 102

Illustration 103

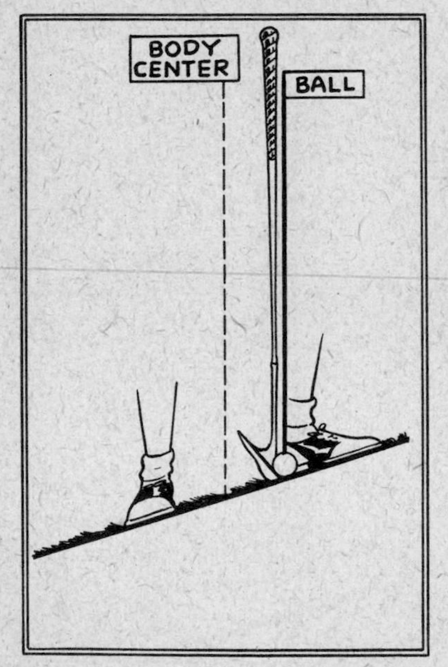

Illustration 104a

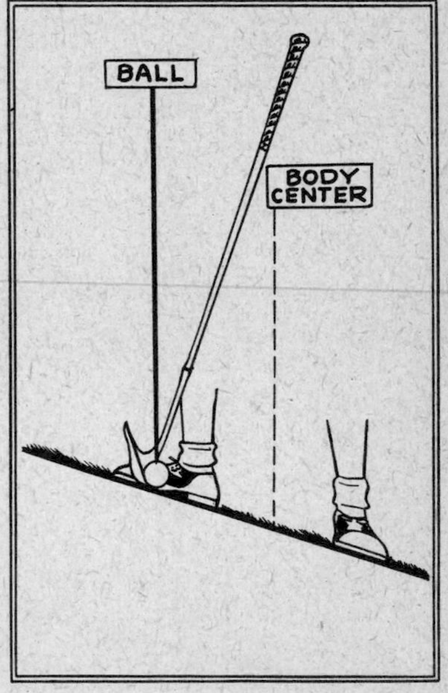

Illustration 104b

Unusual Lies

No matter how well or how carefully you play golf, you are going to frequently find yourself in a position in which you must play the ball in a different manner than you normally do from a level or fairly level lie.

The four broad categories are:

1. UPHILL LIE (Illustration 104a, 105a). Play the ball from approximately the center of your stance. Your weight will naturally be more on the right foot because it is lower than the left (for a right-handed golfer). Use a club with less loft than you would for a shot of the same distance from a level lie. This is necessary because the uneven distribution of weight back on the right foot will cause the ball to get unusually high loft. Most golfers generally hook from this position, so it wise to allow for this hook.

2. DOWNHILL LIE (Illustration 104b, 105b). In this situation I play the ball off my right foot and use an "open" stance. Most of the weight will be on the left foot because of the downhill slope. This time I will select a club with more loft than I would use from a

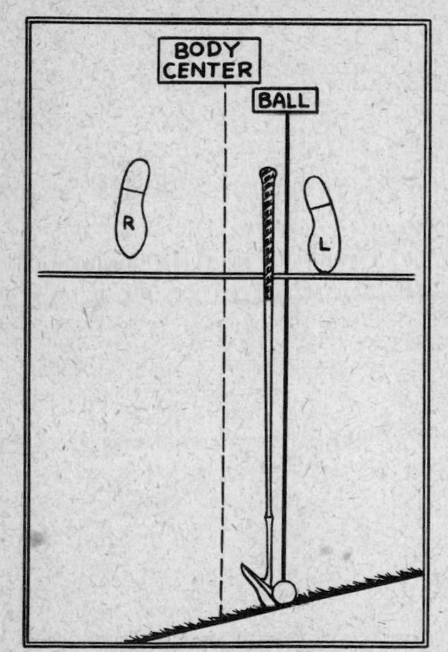

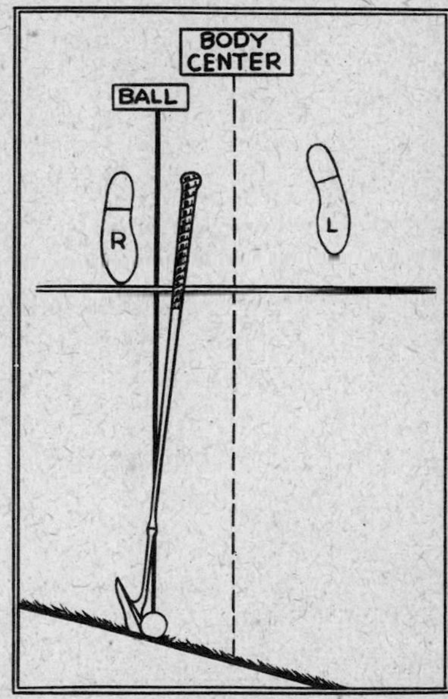

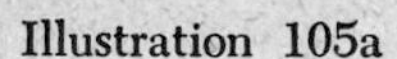
Illustration 105a

Illustration 105b

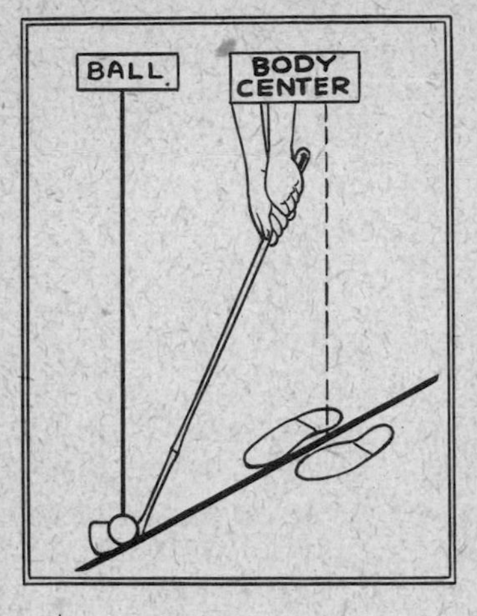

Illustration 106a

Illustration 106b

level lie, otherwise it will have too low a trajectory.

3. SIDEHILL LIE WITH BALL *BELOW* FEET (Illustration 106a). Because I am now standing above the ball and must reach down to it, I move closer than I would for a normal shot from a level lie. Because I cannot get as much power into my swing from this position I will have to use a less lofted club to get the same distance. I play the ball from a point opposite the center of my stance. The tendency is to slice the ball so I make allowances for a slice. I do *not* grip the club right up to the top of the shaft, as might be supposed.

4. SIDEHILL LIE WITH BALL *ABOVE* FEET (Illustration 106b). Now I shorten the grip on the club, usually about as much as the difference in elevation between my feet and the ball. I play the ball from a point back of the center of a slightly "open" stance. You must pay special attention here to taking the club back away from the ball as much on the line of flight as possible, for the tendency is to let it drop to the inside of this imaginary line between the ball and your objective. The average golfer commonly hooks from this lie. If this is true in your case, allow for this hook. Because of the shortened grip I will select a less lofted club than I would in trying to get the same distance from a level lie.

10

The Common Faults of Golf

WHILE A GOOD GOLF SWING IS NOT A NATURAL MOTION, I MAINTAIN that it is basically simple. It becomes complicated only when people try to get too technical about it. The golf swing is a continuous, rhythmic, flowing motion, and *not* a series of unrelated components as is the impression of so many golfers who have been exposed to diversified bad advice.

It is not surprising that confusion exists in the minds of players who have had scores of "do's" and "don'ts" thrust upon them from many sources. The result of this is that they become conscious of many individual body movements throughout the swing, and fail to think of the swing as a single unit. Under these circumstances it is easy to understand why so many people regard golf as a complicated physical activity.

In the vocabulary of the average-to-poor golfer there are two errors which account for all missed shots. One is, "You looked up," or "You took your eye off the ball." The other is, "You tried to kill it."

These faults admittedly do account for many errors. However, these brief analyses are so general that they fail to pin-point the actual mistake. Because of this, the remedy for the actual ill remains a mystery to the afflicted.

While desiring to keep our approach to a study of golf as simple as possible, I do want to present some of the more common faults which plague many players. My purpose is to help those of you who may have developed some bad swinging habits to recognize them so you may more fully benefit from the cures we are about to suggest for each of the more prevalent faults.

If you are a newcomer to the game and have not as yet acquired these afflictions, it would be best for you to by-pass the following discussion of faults (at least until you develop some, if you do — heaven forbid). It may serve only to confuse and scare you.

Placement of Feet

As a generality, we advocate assuming a stance in which balance and comfort are combined to best advantage.

However, it seems that this generality is not enough. Some people imagine that they are comfortable and in good balance when their feet are spread either too far apart or are too close together.

FEET TOO FAR APART – In Illustration 107 my feet are definitely too far apart. This causes a tendency to tighten up, thus restricting freedom of motion in taking the clubhead back from the ball at the start of the backswing. A secondary result of this restriction is to cause you to pick the clubhead up from the ball rather than take it away in a free-swinging motion.

FEET TOO CLOSE TOGETHER – In Illustration 108 we see the opposite extreme in placement of the feet. They are too close together. The consequence is that the person in this position feels top-heavy. It is just as though a tall building had too small a foundation. The left side firmness so essential to a sound swing (in coming in to the ball with the clubhead) is lacking. It is virtually impossible to keep from swaying. The tendency is to pick up the clubhead because of inability to shift the weight properly back on to the right foot.

FEET AS THEY SHOULD BE – With the feet properly spaced, the distance between them is approximately the same as the width of the shoulders. This is a simple and effective rule for determining the proper width of anyone's stance.

My toes are pointed slightly outward to facilitate the freedom of movement in the knees and hips so necessary to executing a good body turn during the swing.

Tension

There is a widespread tendency on the part of golfers to confuse "tension" with "firmness."

In Illustration 109 I am demonstrating exaggerated tension both

Illustration 107

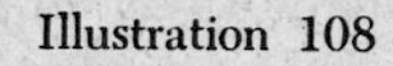

Illustration 108

Illustration 109

Illustration 110

in gripping the club and in standing up to the ball. As unnatural as I may appear to anyone with ever a rudimentary understanding of golf, there are many golfers who stand up to the ball just as I am doing, without realizing that they are over-tense.

My knees are bowed backwards, but this fact is hidden by my skirt. In this position the knees are "locked" or "frozen," thus restricting the normal knee action that takes place in the act of pivoting correctly.

My weight is back on the heels, as is usual with anyone standing rigid or tense at the address. In this position, there is a tendency to rock away from he ball before the swing even begins.

Virtually all the muscles in the body of a person addressing the ball as in this illustration are tied up. Because of this it is impossible for the wrists, arms, or shoulders to function properly. The strain leads to fatigue of both mind and muscles.

CAUSE OF TENSION OR RIGIDITY – Lack of confidence in one's ability to hit the ball is the most common cause of tension or rigidity. To put it another way, FEAR is the leading cause.

The mistaken idea that a very tight grip on the club will increase distance is another cause of tension. Actually, too tight a grip cuts down clubhead speed, for it destroys proper coordination and timing of the swing.

Faults in Starting Clubhead Away from Ball

PICKING UP CLUBHEAD WITH RIGHT HAND – Many golfers want to hit the ball too hard. This leads to jerking the clubhead back away from the ball with the right hand at the start of the backswing. See Illustration 110. The result of this improper motion (in which the right hand predominates) is to curtail the transfer of weight from the left to the right foot – a necessity in any good golfswing . Because it is overpowered by the right hand, the left hand, which is the *guide* hand in the golf swing, never gets a chance to perform its function properly. Consequently the club face has little chance to meet the ball squarely, for the face will likely be open or closed at impact with the ball.

We have referred to the "ideal" golf swing before as a rhythmic, continuous, flowing motion. When the clubhead is jerked up from the ball (as I am demonstrating in Illustration 123) this continuous motion is destroyed, and the swing is broken down into several sections.

DRAGGING CLUBHEAD BACK WITH RIGHT HAND – This is the opposite extreme of the act of *picking* the clubhead up with the right hand, as just discussed.

There is a tendency for those guilty of this fault to pull with the shoulders to help the hands, and "rubber wrists" *drag* the clubhead away from the ball (see Illustration 111). It is generally true that people doing as I am in Illustration 111 feel that they are very deliberately taking the clubhead away from the ball in a low, straight trajectory. Actually, they are taking the clubhead back outside the line of flight with the result that they cut across the ball as they come in to it with the clubhead and get a very bad slice.

TAKING CLUBHEAD AWAY PROPERLY – When I swing correctly, I start the clubhead away from the ball *properly*. I am firm, but not tense. The *left hand is in control.* Remember this always, for it is *vitally important*. My weight is transferring from the left to the right side as it properly should, but there is definitely no *swaying* of the hips or head. My left knee is beginning to flex to

Illustration 111

Illustration 112

accommodate the first stage in the body turn (pivot). There is no unnatural strain or stress. Everything is working together – hands, arms, hips, shoulders, legs, and feet.

Overswing

A very prevalent, and yet erroneous concept among golfers is that the longer the backswing the greater the distance attained in hitting the ball. A proper backswing is governed by extending the left arm as far as it will go comfortably in guiding the clubhead in the proper arc. Those who attempt to lengthen their backswing thinking that they are generating more power are actually extending themselves. The result is that they loosen their hold on the club shaft with their fingers and lose control of the backward course of the club (as demonstrated in Illustration 112). Once the fingers relax to lose control in the backswing, it is impossible to regain control and to bring the clubhead back on the correct arc and in good timing.

The position in which I am shown in Illustration 112 is commonly referred to as a "collapse" at the top of the backswing. It is certainly this, and for all practical purposes it is a collapse of the entire swing. If the clubhead meets the ball squarely after this loss of control at the top of the backswing, it is entirely accidental.

The usual result of getting out of kilter in this manner is to throw the clubhead as the hands suddenly tighten on the shaft in a nattempt to regain the proper grip and control. Consequently the clubhead is thrown outside the line of flight, causing it to cut across the ball and thus impart a slice.

Another possible consequence of lost control at the top is to subconsciously try to compensate for this mistake by turning the right hand over suddenly just before clubhead contact with the ball. A pull or pronounced hook results.

Hands and Body Leading the Clubhead

Here is another fault that stems from the attempt to hit the ball too hard. It can also result from trying to "steer" the ball. What takes place is that the body uncoils too soon, and gets ahead of the clubhead in the course of the downswing. (See Illustration 113.)

As this happens the weight shifts prematurely from the right over to the left foot.

My shoulders and head have moved out of position in front of the ball, as can be seen in Illustration 113. Because my head is the hub about which my swing revolves, the whole swing has moved forward out of the originally-intended arc.

The usual consequence of this fault is a shot that is hit on the neck of the club and pushed off to the right. A "shanked shot" which angles off unexpectedly and sharply to the right may also result.

Hitting Behind the Ball

There are several reasons for people's hitting behind the ball. However, the most common is trying to "scoop" or help the ball into the air. This causes a chopping motion in which the hands lead the clubhead down too fast .

In the theoretically perfect swing, the left arm and the shaft of the club form a straight line from the left shoulder to the ball at

Illustration 113 Illustration 114

the time of clubhead impact with the ball. The key point in this faulty action is shown in Illustration 114. You will note that because my hands have come through too fast they are ahead of the clubhead. I have thus led the clubhead down into the ground, rather than into the back of the ball.

This same urge to get the blade of the club *under* the ball also often leads to a "dipping" action in the knees, with the result that the whole arc of the swing is lowered. The consequence is obvious. The club will meet the turf behind the ball, and a good old-fashioned "dub" or "scuff" will follow.

Topping the Ball

A topped shot is usually the result of "rearing" or leaning back from the ball just before the moment of impact, as I am demonstrating in Illustration 115. Note that I have settled back on my heels forcing the club up and around my body. In the process of doing this I move the position of my feet to keep from falling backward. My weight has remained back on my right foot, rather than shifted

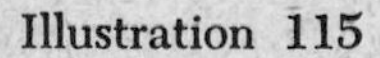

Illustration 115 Illustration 116

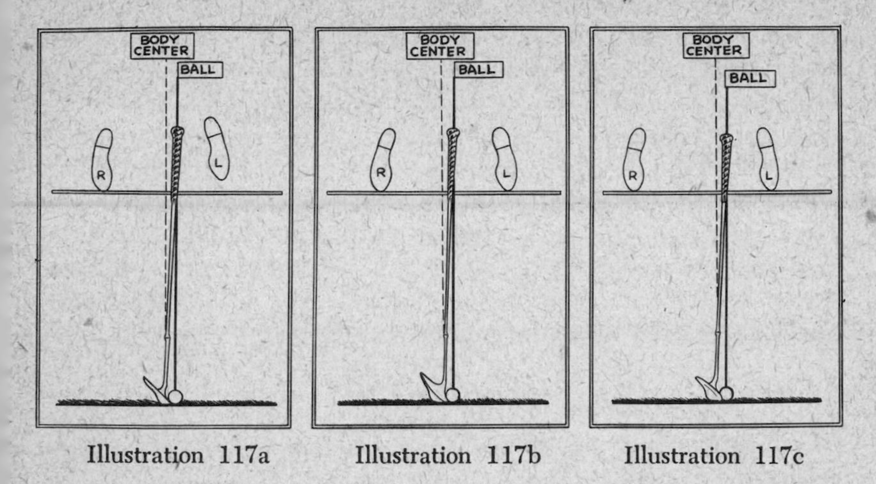

Illustration 117a Illustration 117b Illustration 117c

over to my left as it should, with the start of the downswing. This is because I was so intent on hitting the ball *real* hard that I just flailed at it without regard for proper timing. Thus I had no chance to meet the ball squarely.

Another common cause of topping the ball is looking at the very top of the ball rather than at the back of the ball. And the human body seems so constructed that you will hit the point on which you are concentrating.

The Slice

A slice (flight starting to the left and curving to the right) is generally caused by the hands getting in ahead of the clubhead with the result that the club face is open (laying back as shown in Illustrations 116 and 117b) upon contact with the ball.

However, there are many different causes of a slice. One is an open stance. When your feet are in a too open stance (see Illustration 8b) it is impossible to swing the club back in a normal arc because the position of the right foot (back of the line of the left) causes a blocking of the right hip. When this happens the clubhead goes back in what is seemingly a straight line from the ball, but because of the blocked position it actually goes *outside* the line of flight (see Illustration 118). Because the clubhead usually comes down in the same arc in which it was taken back from the ball (unless control is lost at the top), it will travel from the outside

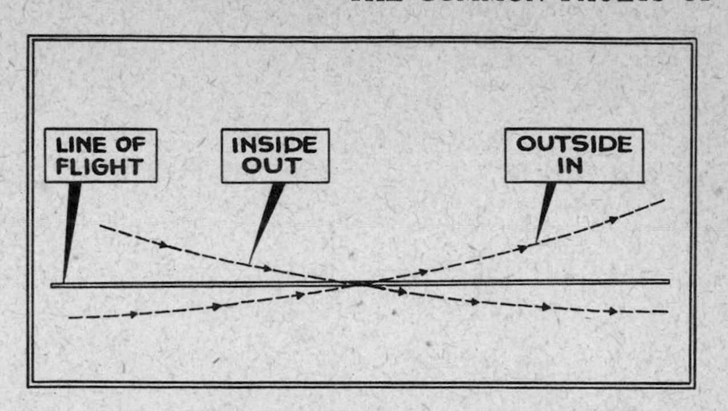

Illustration 118

to the inside across the line of flight as it meets the ball. A slice is certain to follow.

Another fault which can lead to a sliced shot is that of placing the right hand too far over the shaft to the left so that the hands are working against one another. (See Illustration 3 for proper position of right hand). This will usually cause picking the club up with the resulting ills that we have already discussed earlier in this chapter under the heading of "Picking Clubhead up with Right Hand."

The Hook

The hooked shot is the reverse of a slice. The ball starts out to the right of the line of flight and curves back to the left.

The most common cause of a hook is a club face which is shutting or shut (see Illustrations 119 and 117c) at the moment of impact. The reason for this is that we roll the right hand back or under the club shaft as we take the clubhead back *inside* the line of flight (see Illustration 118). To get the hands back into the same position they were in at address they must roll during the downswing. The natural tendency is to roll them too much with the result that the club face is shutting (as mentioned above) at impact. A hook is the only possible consequence.

A closed stance as demonstrated in Illustration 8c is a frequent cause of a hooked ball. In drawing the right foot back from the line of flight as shown (see Illustration 8c) I have set the stage for an accentuated turn of the body to the right. This in turn causes

Illustration 119 Illustration 120

the clubhead to travel in an arc around the body on a flatter plane than normal. As the clubhead returns to the ball via this same arc and plane, the left side, because it is advanced more than the right toward the ball, tends to prevent the arms and hands from swinging through toward the intended objective. This is called "blocking." The sub-conscious result of the knowledge that you are aiming to the right (because of the closed stance) and must get the ball around to the left, causes most golfers to roll their wrists over with the results described above.

It is possible through adequate compensation or corrective action with the hands to bring the club face squarely into the ball despite the faults in the backswing. Sometimes when this adjustment or correction is perfectly timed, a straight ball results, but this is usually accidental.

While the hook and the slice are admittedly the result of faulty swinging with a golf club, there is a place for both. You may find yourself in such a position that only by hooking or slicing can you reach your desired objective.

As a final word of caution – never allow yourself to accept a hook or slice as your inescapable fate. Any qualified teaching professional can remedy the causes of these ailments in your swing in surprisingly short order, that is with at least a fair amount of indulgence or application on your part.

Finishing Off Balance

Finishing in an unnatural, off-balance position, as Illustration 120 shows, is the result of slugging at the ball. Just before clubhead contact with the ball I pulled my head and shoulders up and out of their original position. Instead of the hands' finishing at least head high as they should (see Illustration 32), they have dropped shoulder-high much in the manner of the finish of a baseball swing. This is the result of improperly swinging the club away from the ball as one would in "winding up" to hit a baseball out of the park. The club has travelled in somewhat the same plane as does a baseball bat just before impact.

Instead of the clubhead's being taken back smoothly and firmly on the line of flight, chances are that it has been jerked away by the right hand. This leads to what is generally known as the "flat swing" in which the clubhead revolves in an arc on the same plane as the shoulders. In other words, the shoulders are the hub about which the arms revolve, and the swing becomes a circular motion around the body. This leads to finishing the swing in an off-balance position as shown in Illustration 120. Note how I am far off balance, with the weight way over on the left side of my left foot, and the toe of my right foot barely on the ground. See Illustration 32 for proper foot position at the conclusion of the swing. Here there has been a general collapse of every swinging component in this swing as demonstrated in Illustration 120.

Out of this faulty swing the mistakes most likely to happen are (1) topped balls, (2) hooks, (3) slices, and a number of varied high and low-skimming shots depending upon the degree to which the flatness and the revolving arc are accentuated.

11

Club Selection in the "Scoring Zone"

THE BEST GOLF SWING IN THE WORLD CAN BE NULLIFIED BY A WRONG choice of clubs for specific shots.

It is especially important in the so-called "scoring zone" within easy short iron distance of the green to use the club best suited to the particular situation in which the golfer finds himself. Upon the choice of clubs may very well depend the success or failure of such a shot. The less experienced player, in particular, may waste anywhere from six to 20 strokes in a single round merely by taking the wrong club out of the bag for a shot intended to get the ball up close to the pin.

A recent Men's National Open was lost by a player who chose to use a putter from five feet off the green. The ball rolled well past the pin and he missed the putt coming back. That single stroke cost him a tie for the title. The "second-guessers" really had a field day in replaying this shot after the tournament was over. The wisdom of this great star's choice was debated for some time. Naturally, because he "blew" the shot, the consensus was that he should have used a lofted club.

It is impossible to lay down a hard and fast set of rules to fit every possible situation encountered around the greens, but I believe I can be helpful, particularly to the inexpert player, in demonstrating the clubs I have found to be most efficient in playing some of the more commonly encountered approach shots.

Approaching with a Putter

In Illustrations A-1, A-2, and A-3 you see me employing a putter in an attempt to roll the ball up to the pin from a point about a

Illustration A–1

Illustration A–2 Illustration A–3

foot off the edge of the green and on level terrain. I believe it is a gamble to use a putter off the fairway grass when the ball is much more than a foot away from the green, for it is difficult to determine just how much resistance the ball will meet from the longer fairway grass.

The stroke I employ for a shot such as the one illustrated here is a simple putting stroke with the ball being played from a point off my left foot. Details of this stroke are covered in the chapter on putting.

Uphill Chip to Pin

In the shot situation illustrated in panorama Picture B-1 my long shot to the green has fallen a couple of yards short of the putting surface. The pin is well back on the green, as you can see.

The ball will have to travel only a short distance in the air to clear the fairway grass and land on the green, yet it must roll a considerable distance after landing. Thus my choice of clubs here is a No. 6 iron, for it will best suit the situation at hand – short carry plus long roll against an uphill slope.

Illustration B–1

Illustration B–2

Illustration B–3

Illustration B–4

Illustration B–5

Illustration C–1

Illustration C–2 Illustration C–3

Illustration C–4 Illustration C–5

We have covered the details of the swing employed in playing short irons earlier in the book, so I will endeavor here only to show you the stance for this shot (Illustration B-2) and the length of the swing (Illustrations B-3 and B-5), plus my position at impact with the ball (Illustration B-4). In a similar situation but from 5 yards or so farther out I would use a No. 7 iron.

Downhill Chip to Pin

As pictured in Illustration C-1 my ball is about two yards off the edge of the green, which slopes gently away from me down to the pin, which is about 20 feet from the edge of the green. The ball rests in long grass just barely in the rough.

My problem here is to get the ball over the fairway grass and have it light on the green with a minimum of forward momentum so that it will not roll past the pin. This means I must hit a more rapidly ascending and descending shot than in playing the chip shot previously discussed. Consequently, I choose a lofted club which in this case is a No. 8 iron. A short, firm swing is employed as you see in Pictures C-2 through C-5. Picture C-4 illustrates the sharp ascent of the ball so essential to limiting the roll after it lands.

As pictured in Illustration D-1, I find myself in a situation where the terrain breaks sharply away from me down to the cup, with the edge of the green about halfway between me and the pin, which is only 18 feet distant. It is imperative that the ball clear the long grass and have enough loft and "bite" or backspin on it so that it will stop quickly after landing on the green. To achieve this end I am using a No. 9 iron as demonstrated in Illustrations D-2 through D-5.

Pitch Shot to Front Edge of Green

In the situation pictured in Illustration E-1, I am back about 20 yards from the pin, which is close to the front edge of the green. The grass in front of the green is fairly long and the ground is somewhat bumpy. Hence, it would be unwise to try to light the ball short of the green and have it run up to the hole. My best bet is to play the ball so that it will land on the green and yet not overrun the hole.

Illustration D–1

Illustration D–2

Illustration D–3

Illustration D–4

Illustration D–5

To accomplish this I must use a club with the most lofted face of any club in my bag. This is the *pitching wedge,* which is specifically designed for this very purpose. It will impart a sharply-rising and descending trajectory to the flight of the ball and will also cause a brisk backspin on the ball, which may be accentuated by swinging in an outside-in arc, which causes the blade to cut across under the ball.

To play this shot I assume an "open" stance as you see in Illustration E-2. The club is placed on the ground to make clear the extent of this openness. The shaft of this club represents the line of flight.

Because most of the momentum of the swing is spent in giving loft or elevation to the flight of the ball, it is necessary to employ a fairly full backswing as you see in Pictures E-3 through E-5. Even though this is a rather short shot, I follow through with the clubhead to about the same extent as the length of the backswing. The majority of the higher handicap players neglect this all-important follow through.

Pitching Over An Osbstacle to the Pin

The presence of an obstacle such as a yawning sand trap between ball and pin often causes the average player to get "buck fever" or to "choke up" because of more concern over the consequences of a missed shot than over playing the shot properly.

Ironically, the low handicap player to whom a shot situation such as that portrayed in Illustration F-1 is "just another shot," seldom finds himself in this predicament. It is the less expert golfer who has a tendency to stray in his efforts to hit the green. Consequently he or she is the one who most frequently encounters the need for playing out of a trouble spot such as we see here.

My ball is buried in fairly long grass. I must get it out of this grass cleanly and yet with enough forward momentum so that it will carry over the trap, sharply enough up into the air and with backspin so that it will stop short upon hitting the green.

The club that will best achieve the desired result here is the *pitching wedge.* By using this club and swinging it in an outside-in line designed to make it cut across from right-to-left under the ball, I can cause the ball to rise sharply as it does in Picture F-4 and also

Illustration E–1

Illustration E–2

Illustration E–3

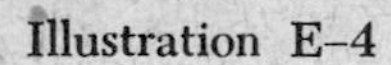

Illustration E–4

Illustration E–5

Illustration F–1

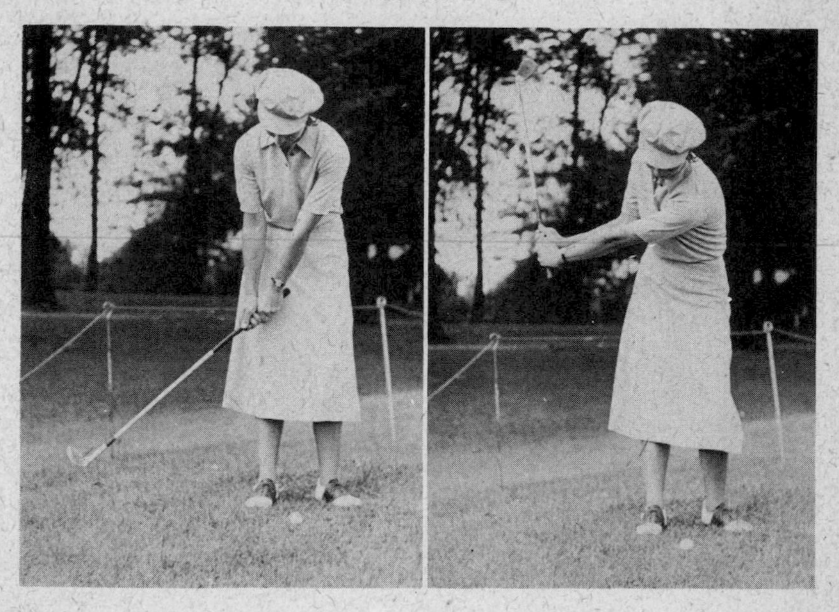

Illustration F–2

Illustration F–3

Illustration F–4

Illustration F–5

impart the backspin necessary to make the ball stop short after it lands on the green. Illustration F-3 gives you an idea of the extent of the backswing and follow through employed in playing this shot. Don't let this shot scare you. You'll be surprised at the ease with which you can master it after a little practice.

Chip Shot to Green from Long Grass in Trap or Bunker

Again, because the higher handicap players have difficulty in hitting the greens consistently on their longer shots to the green, they must often play from the grassy slopes of a bunker or trap and try to get the ball up close to the pin.

Uphill Slope

If I have an uphill lie such as the one in Illustration G-1, I will probably use a No. 7 iron and play it off my left foot as demonstrated. The combination of the uphill lie and the natural loft of the No. 7 iron will be sufficient to get the ball into the air high

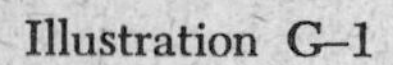

Illustration G–1

Illustration G–2

Illustration G–3

Illustration G–4

Illustration H–1

Illustration H–2

Illustration H–3 Illustration H–4

enough to clear the mound before me. In this particular case the pin is in the center of the green, so there is no need to stop the ball abruptly after it lands on the green. Of course, if the cup were very close to my side of the green, I would have to use a more lofted club to cut down the roll after the ball hit the green.

The swing for this shot is fairly short (yet firm) as you see in Illustrations G-2 through G-4.

Downhill Slope

Even the more expert players sometimes find themselves on the downhill slope of a mound, trap, or bunker to the side or back of the green at which they are shooting.

When I find myself in this situation, I select a more lofted and deep-faced club (a No. 9 iron in the instance demonstrated here) and play the ball off a point opposite my *right* foot as in Illustration H-1. The more lofted club is needed to get the ball up into the air so that it will land on the green, yet not have too much forward momentum.

Here again the swing is short but bold, as you can see in studying Pictures H-2 through H-4. Note particularly in Illustration H-3 how my hands are well ahead of the clubhead as it approaches and makes contact with the ball. There is a very common tendency to "chop" or "stab" at the ball in playing this shot. Be *sure* you follow through firmly.

12

Conclusion

HAVING ENLARGED UPON THE VARIOUS MECHANICS INVOLVED IN THE golf swing in the preceding chapters, I cannot resist inserting a few random remarks concerning the game of golf itself while I still have such an excellent opportunity to make myself heard.

At the outset, however, I would like to assure all lovers of tennis, swimming, or whatever sport may be the particular favorite that this is not intended as a piece of propaganda advocating golf as "the king of sports."

I can hardly deny that this is my own personal feeling, but my immediate objective here is simply to speak further of the pleasant and sometimes infuriating aspects of this sport which I particularly love after a long and intimate association with it.

We have come to know each other quite well – Golf and I – and we get along famously for the most part, although, like friends, we get on the "outs" with each other once in a while. There are days when it seems that I "can't make a nickel" and I would like to think that golf is a fickle friend unworthy of my loyalty and devotion. But when I stop to think the whole thing out, I know that there could never be a more steadfast friend nor one who could possibly teach me more valuable lessons in the art of living.

The greatest single lesson to be learned from playing golf, I think, is that of controlling one's thinking and emotions – mental discipline – which is of prime importance in the business of getting along with oneself and with others. The player who sincerely desires to progress in golf eventually discovers that displays of anger and impatience, however satisfying to her feelings at the time, merely thwart her hopes for decent scores. She learns to swallow her shame at having dubbed her first tee shot under the scrutiny of the usual onlookers and to ignore the seven she collected on the par three fifth hole after having been even par up to that point.

That considerable time elapses between shots in golf allows not only for mental torture about poor shots that have already been executed, but also for a great play by the fertile imagination as to the possible outcome of the shots that are yet to come. The prospect of having to shoot across a lengthy water hazard to the green, for example, can often present harrowing mental pictures to the player before she has even walked up to the ball. By the time she is ready to execute the shot, her mind is so filled with apprehension that she cannot possibly do justice to the shot.

Because of this need for mental discipline, the player soon develops the ability to accept rather than resent situations which arise. In other words, she learns that she must face things as they come, readjust her plans to suit the circumstances, and go on to the best of her ability from there on in.

The power of concentration may also be developed in playing golf. Many a player kids herself into thinking that the airplane flying overhead or the shadow cast across the line of her putt was the cause of the missed shot, when in reality, the blame cannot be laid to anything outside herself. If she had been totally absorbed in the act of executing the shot, she would not have been aware of the airplane or the shadow — much less allowed these irrelevant factors to dominate her consciousness and to upset her purpose.

Golf, I think then, is a game requiring many of the qualities which are demanded of us every day in successful and happy living. The zealous golfer develops a philosophy which enables her to rise above the "hazards" and "penalties" which occur in her everyday life and aids her in maintaining her equilibrium under any circumstances.

Golf, like life, is a humbling experience, and there is no way in the world for a person to set himself up as its master. As soon as one presumes that he is in complete control of himself and his fate, on the golf course or off, he finds there is a rude awakening. For this notion of personal power is only to be rewarded by its opposite — the harshest realization of the complete powerlessness of personal will to shape or determine the future.

The oft-quoted expression, "the harder I try, the worse I become," illustrates the futile effort to overcome obstacles, be they sandtraps or problems in everyday life, by sheer force of will. Golf is not a game of stress and violent activity, but one requiring mental and physical finesse. It calls for relaxation of mind and muscle rather than the taut vigor of the football player, for instance. The golfer forms the habit of acting with the greatest possible freedom and ease under a given situation and then not fretting about what lies in the future.

And finally, playing golf is so akin to just plain living itself, it seems, because both are essentially a constant battle within the individual. There is no tougher opponent on the golf course than the one inside oneself who says, "you had better not hook this shot because you might end up in that trap to the left of the green." How easy it is to fill the mind with dread of impending failure before the job at hand has even been tackled! The person who succeeds in ignoring the hints of doom suggested by this "voice" within is the person who approaches his goal not only on the fairway but wherever else he may be.

The challenge presented to the individual on the golf course is so similar to the challenge presented by life itself that the game takes on importance to the individual far greater than is to be imagined at first glance. Aside from the enjoyment that is to be derived from participation in an outdoor activity of this kind, golf offers a proving ground for the practice of qualities of character which make for a more serene and well-adjusted life at a time when people are surrounded by tension and pressure.

Index

DISCARD